Instructor's Notebook:
TPR™ Homework Exercises

by

Ramiro Garcia

Author of:

Instructor's Notebook:
How To Apply TPR For Best Results

The Graphics Book
in English, Spanish, French or German

TPR Bingo
in English, Spanish, French or German

edited by

James J. Asher

ISBN: 978-1-56018-004-3

Published by

Sky Oaks Productions, Inc.
P.O. Box 1102
Los Gatos, CA 95031 USA

Phone: (408) 395-7600 • **Fax:** (408) 395-8440
tprworld@aol.com

For fast service, order online at:

www.tpr-world.com

Instructor's Notebook:
TPR Homework Exercises

INTRODUCTION

Here is how you can use <u>this</u> <u>sequel</u> to my book, **The Instructor's Notebook: How To Apply TPR For Best Results**...

- as **homework exercises** to help your students accelerate their stress-free understanding, speaking, reading and writing of any target language,

- as **"catch-up" exercises** for students who have missed one or more classes,

- to **review** the classroom TPR experience in the privacy of their own home,

- to **help other members of the student's family** enjoy a fast-moving, stress-free acquisition of another language, and

- to **help you acquire the native language of the students you are teaching** with my **self-instructional exercises** that will give you he excitement of internalizing another language fast and almost without effort.

SECTION 1: CARTOON STRIPS

This booklet has three sections. In the first section, which you may find is most appropriate for your **beginning students,** you will find a strip of cartoons like this:

Your student at home with an audio cassette listens to you utter a direction in the target language, **"Stand up"** and looks at the first stick figure. Then the student hears you say, **"Sit down,"** while looking at the second stick figure. Then again in the second picture, the student hears you say; **"Stand up"** and **"Sit down."** And in the third picture, once more the student hears you say; **"Stand up"** and **"Sit down."** Now the figure will make another move with **"Stand up,"** and **"Walk"** in the fourth picture. Finally, in the fifth picture; **"Stop"** and then **"Walk."**

Gradually the directions in the target language become more complex until in **Lesson Twelve,** the student hears you say, **"Go to the chalkboard"** and **"Touch the chalkboard."** And further into the lesson, **"Walk to the table and pick up the chair."** Then, **"Put the chair on top of the table."**

SECTION 1: SPEAKING

I have just illustrated how the twelve lessons in **Section 1** can be used to help students acquire listening comprehension of the target language (any target language). But the pictures can also be valuable for **practicing speaking** in the target language. When your students have made the transition to production, they utter a direction in the target language as they look at each picture. If they wish feedback to check their pronunciation, they can simply turn on the audio cassette.

SECTION 1: READING AND WRITING

If you wish your students to **practice writing**, ask them to write a direction for each picture. As they advance in training, encourage them to be more creative in their write-up such as this for the **first picture** in the strip below:

"Why do you have your hands in the air? That is a strange way to stand up from a chair. You look very thin, almost a skeleton. Don't you enjoy eating?"

As to **reading**, pair up your students. Ask them to exchange papers after they have written something novel for each picture in a strip and then have one of the students read aloud what their partner has written in the target language. Reward the most entertaining write-up with a small prize.

SECTION 2: CHAINING

Chaining is a successful technique I have developed to **stretch the student's attention span** for understanding what a native speaker is saying in the target language. For example in the set of pictures in "**A**" below,

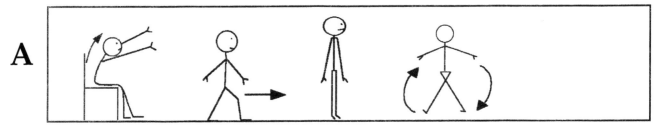

…you utter the following directions rapidly with no pauses: **"Stand up. Walk. Stop. Turn around."** In the classroom, the student must wait until the entire chain is uttered before making a move to perform each direction in the sequence.

You notice that the pictures in row **B** continue the action in row **A**. Gradually, we expand the student's attention span so that we start with four pictures in "**A**" and "**B**", then increase the number of pictures to six in **C**, **D**, and **E**.

SECTION 2: READING AND SPEAKING

If you would like your students to practice reading and speaking, then here is a variation with the chains: Provide your student with the directions in print for the chain in "A." The student reads the directions, then looks at the series of pictures in chain "A."

As another variation, you may ask the student to read aloud each direction before looking at a set of pictures.

SECTION 2: WRITING

For a fun exercise, ask your student to write a story about a set of pictures in a chain. Encourage them to be imaginative, zany, even crazy! Reward the most entertaining story with a small prize. For example, here is a short story for row **A** of **Chain One**.

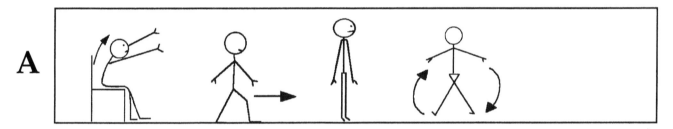

"The boy has a back problem so that it is difficult to stand up. You can see the pain as he raises his hands above his head. Finally he is on his feet and walking. Suddenly, he sees an alligator in the wastebasket. He turns in the opposite direction, screaming for the teacher."

SECTION 3: PICTURE DESCRIPTIONS

For each picture, ask your student in class or at home to write something interesting. Encourage creativity, zaniness, even the weird. Reward the most entertaining write-ups with a small prize.

Here are examples of what your **advanced students** might write for each picture:

"Put your hands up. This is a hold up. Higher! I want your money. Why are you smiling? Why are you not wearing any clothes? Where do you carry your wallet?"

"Put your right hand on the table. Put your left hand on your waist. What are you looking at ? What is so funny?"

"Put your head on the table. Put your hands behind you. Lift your hands in the air. Are you practicing Yoga? Is it helpful to have the blood run to your head?"

"Why is the arrow pointing at your nose? Do you have a cold? I can recommend a good doctor. It is difficult to breath with all the pollutants in the air. I recommend that you move to Santa Fe, New Mexico."

SECTION 1: CARTOON STRIPS

LESSON ONE

SYMBOLS : @ Again   {1,2} Do it twice | Emphasis   {!!} Fast   (•••) Pause   ⟶ Return   ⟳ Slowly   ( ) Turn Around

SECTION 1: CARTOON STRIPS
LESSON TWO

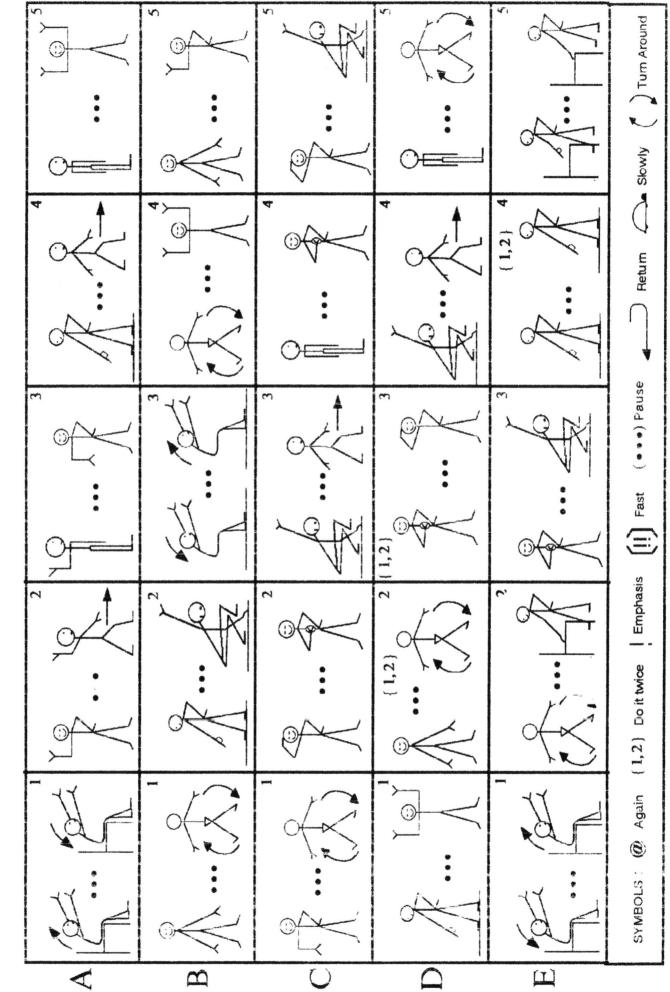

SYMBOLS: @ Again (1,2) Do it twice | Emphasis [!!] Fast (•••) Pause ➤ Return ⌒ Slowly ( ) Turn Around

SECTION 1: CARTOON STRIPS

LESSON THREE

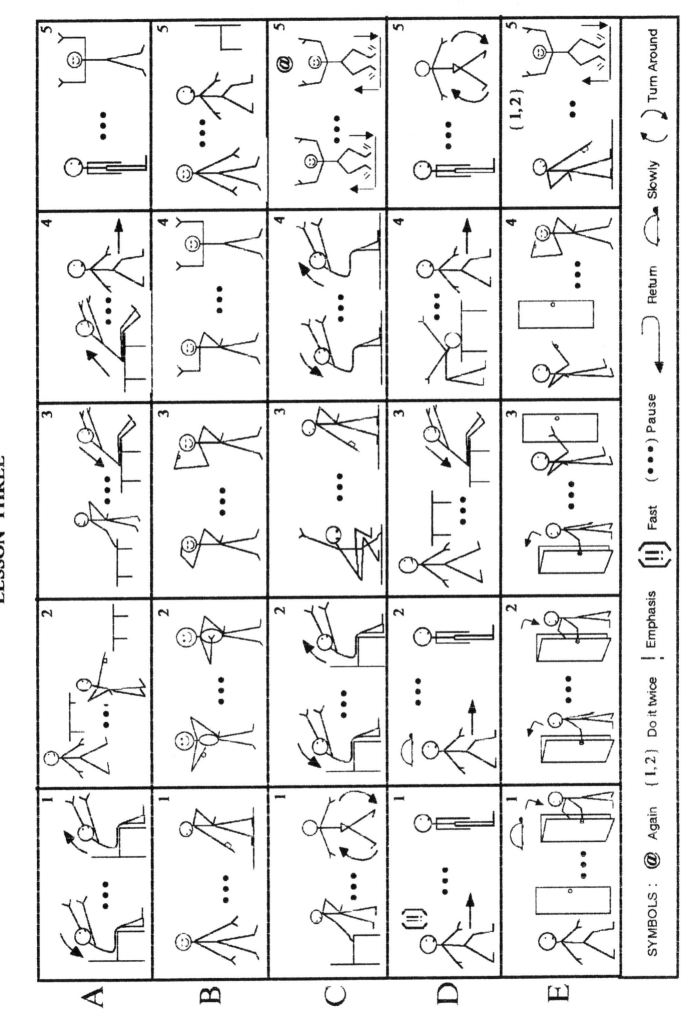

SYMBOLS: @ Again { 1, 2 } Do it twice ! Emphasis (!!) Fast (•••) Pause ⊃ Return ⊃ Slowly ( ) Turn Around

SECTION 1: CARTOON STRIPS

LESSON FOUR

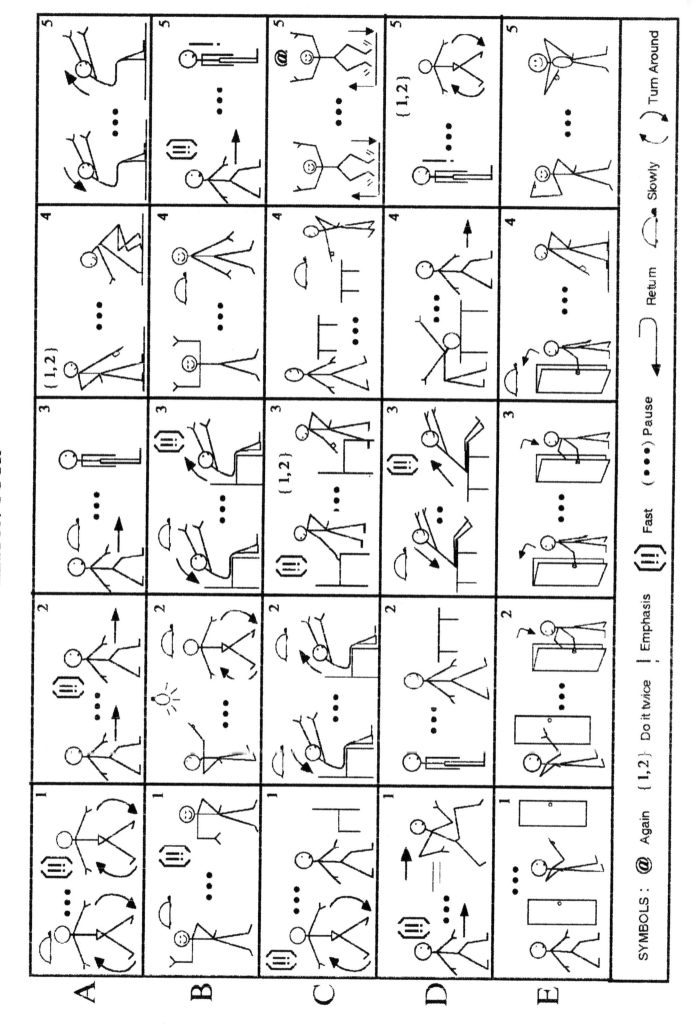

SYMBOLS : @ Again {1,2} Do it twice | Emphasis [!!] Fast (•••) Pause → Return Slowly ↺ Turn Around

SECTION 1: CARTOON STRIPS

LESSON FIVE

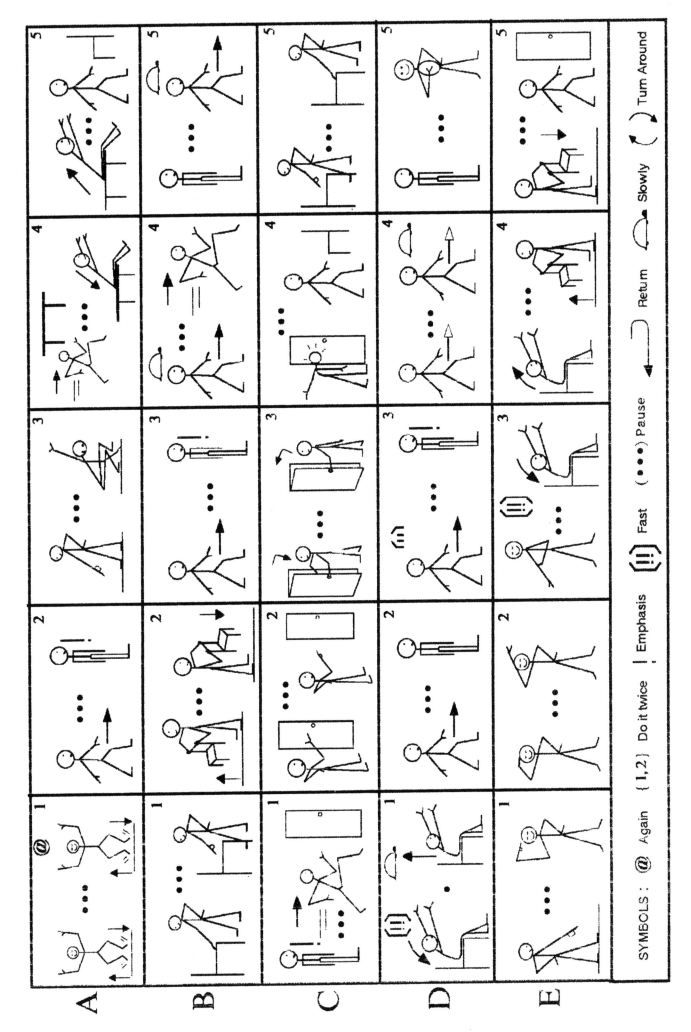

SYMBOLS : @ Again   {1,2} Do it twice | Emphasis   [!!] Fast   (•••) Pause   Return   Slowly   Turn Around

SECTION 1: CARTOON STRIPS

LESSON SIX

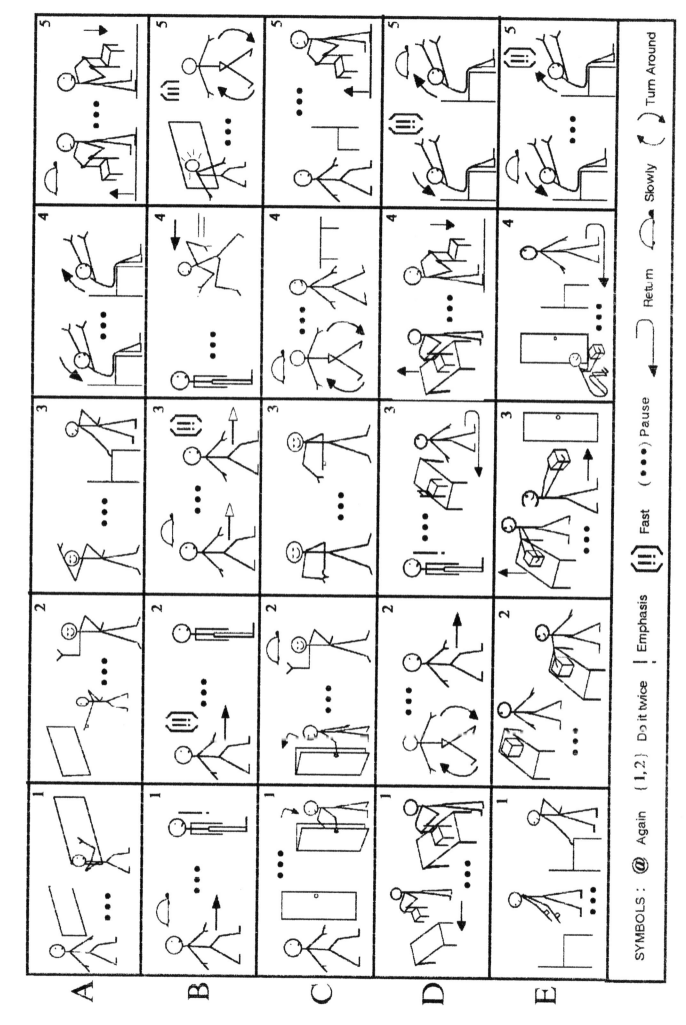

SYMBOLS : @ Again   {1,2} Do it twice | Emphasis   (!) Fast   Return   Slowly   Turn Around

SECTION 1: CARTOON STRIPS

LESSON SEVEN

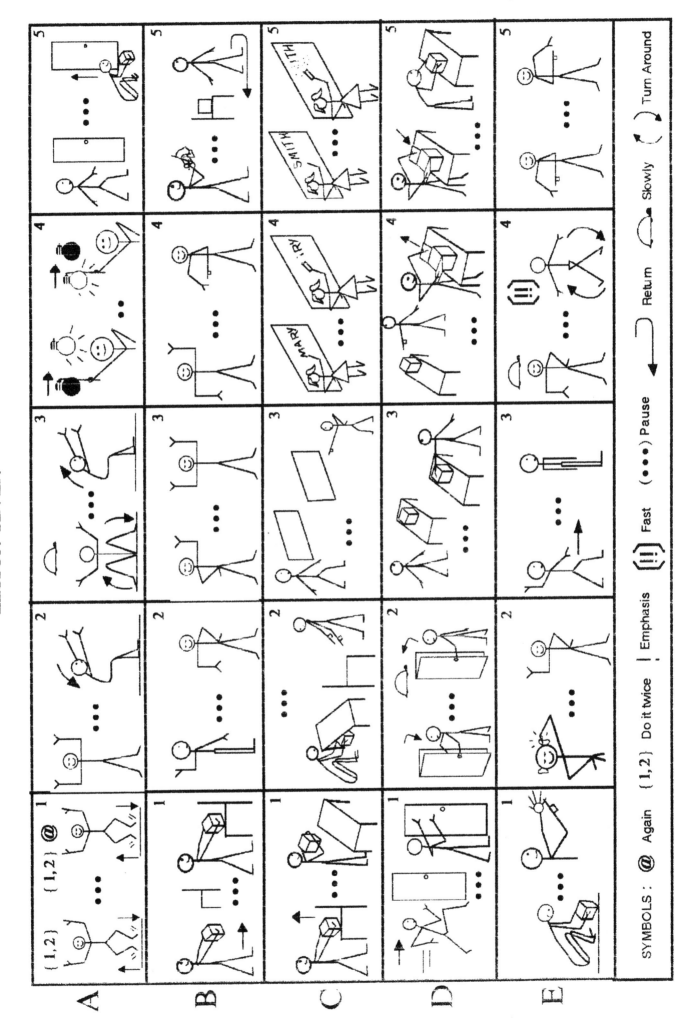

SYMBOLS : @ Again   {1,2} Do it twice   ! Emphasis   [!] Fast   (•••) Pause   Return   Slowly   Turn Around

SECTION 1: CARTOON STRIPS
LESSON EIGHT

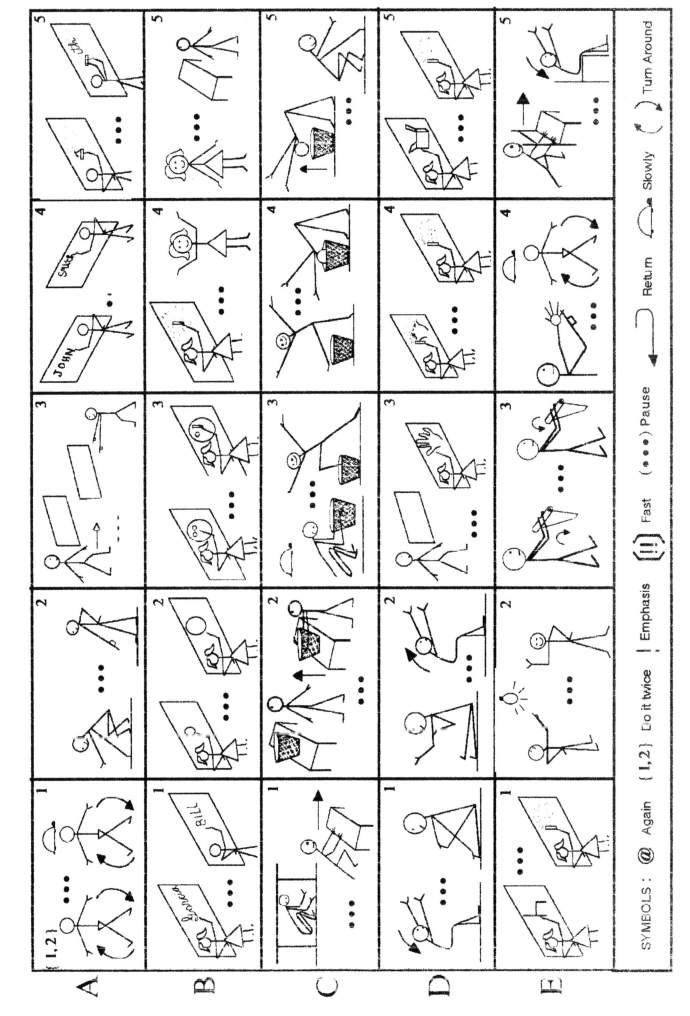

SYMBOLS : @ Again {1,2} Do it twice ! Emphasis [!] Fast (•••) Pause ⟶ Return ⌣ Slowly ( ) Turn Around

SECTION 1: CARTOON STRIPS

LESSON NINE

SYMBOLS : @ Again   {1,2} Do it twice   ! Emphasis   [!!] Fast   (•••) Pause   ⟶ Return   ◠ Slowly   ( ) Turn Around

SECTION 1: CARTOON STRIPS

LESSON TEN

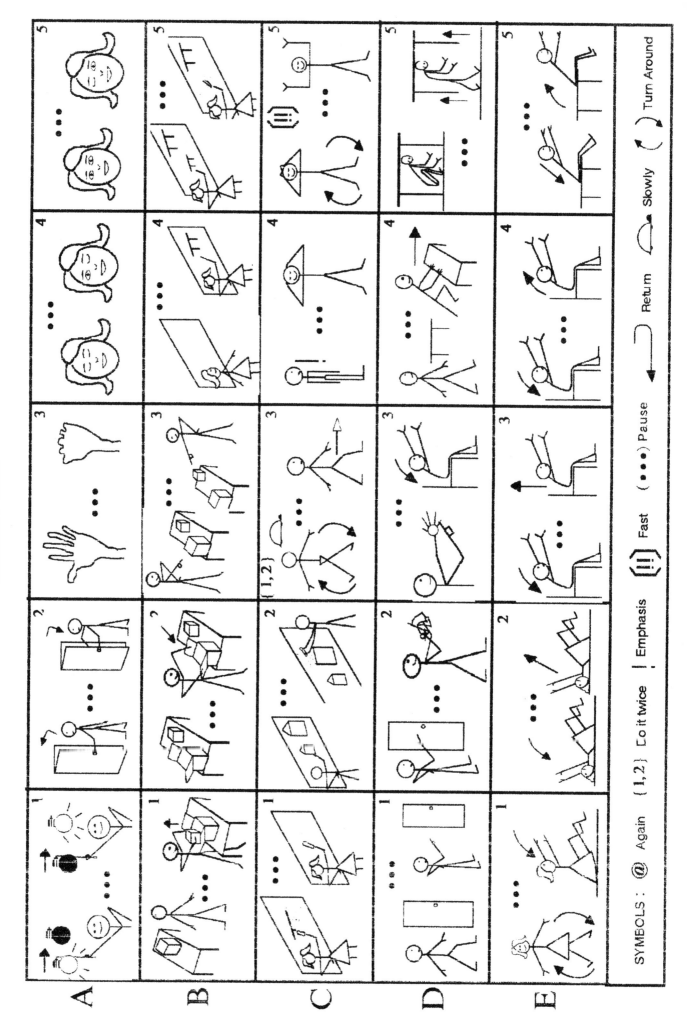

SYMBOLS : @ Again   (1,2) Do it twice | Emphasis   [!!] Fast   (•••) Pause   ⌣ Return   ⌢ Slowly   ( ) Turn Around

SECTION 1: CARTOON STRIPS
LESSON ELEVEN

SYMBOLS : @ Again {1,2} Do it twice | Emphasis [!!] Fast (•••) Pause ⌐ Return ⌢ Slowly ( ) Turn Around

SECTION 1: CARTOON STRIPS

LESSON TWELVE

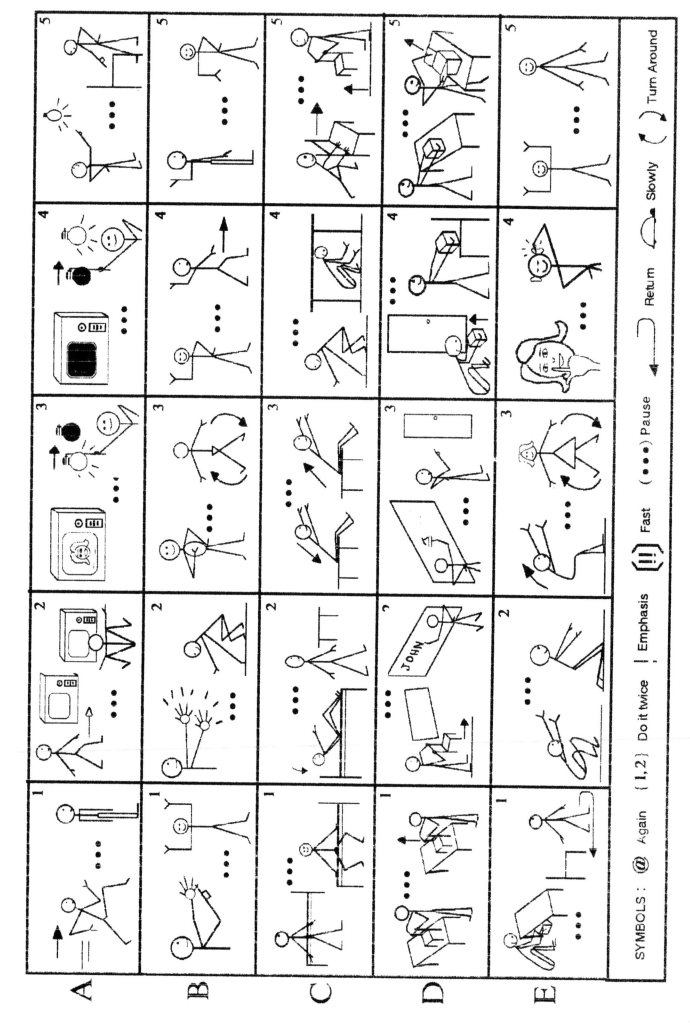

SYMBOLS : ⓐ Again   { 1, 2 } Do it twice | Emphasis   ⟦!!⟧ Fast   ⌣ Return   ⌢ Slowly   ( ) Turn Around   (•••) Pause

Guidelines
for recording the teacher's voice on the audio cassette

Let's start with Lesson One. Your student at home looks at the first picture in Row A which shows a person standing up and then sitting down. The student hears on an audio cassette that you have made in the target language, **"Lesson one. Row A. Picture one. Get up"**... (SHORT PAUSE)...**"Sit down."**

The second picture again shows a person standing up and then sitting down. You say on the audio cassette in the target language, **"Picture two. Get up"**... (SHORT PAUSE)...**"Sit down."**

The third picture once again shows a person standing up and then sitting down. You say on the audio cassette in the target language, **"Picture three. Get up"**...(SHORT PAUSE)... **"Sit down."**

The fourth picture in Row A shows a person standing up, then walking. The student hears you say on the audio cassette in the target language, **"Picture four. Get up"**...(SHORT PAUSE) ... **"Walk."**

In the fifth picture in Row A, the person stops and then walks. Your student looks at the pictures as he or she hears you say, **"Picture five. Stop"** ...(SHORT PAUSE)...**"Walk."**

Now that the student understands how the pattern works, I recommend that you discontinue using the word **"Picture."** Simply say, **"Lesson one. Row B. One. Walk"**...(SHORT PAUSE)...**"Stop."**

"Two. Walk"...(SHORT PAUSE)...**"Stop."**

"Three. Turn around"...(SHORT PAUSE)...**"Turn around again."**

"Four. Turn around"...(SHORT PAUSE)... **"Turn around again."**

"Five. Walk"...(SHORT PAUSE)...**"Stop."**

On the following pages, you will find the script for Lesson One through Lesson Twelve.

SECTION 1: CARTOON STRIPS

LESSON ONE

Row A
1. Get up ... Sit down
2. Get up ... Sit down
3. Get up ... Sit down
4. Get up ... Walk
5. Stop ... Walk

Row B
1. Walk ... Stop
2. Walk ... Stop
3. Turn around ... Turn around again
4. Turn around ... Turn around again
5. Walk ... Stop

Row C
1. Turn around ... Sit down
2. Get up ... Turn around
3. Turn around ... Walk
4. Stop ... Sit down
5. Get up ... Turn around

Row D
1. Turn around again ... Walk
2. Stop ... Walk
3. Stop ... Turn around
4. Raise your arm ... Put your arm down
5. Raise your arm again ... Put your arm down

Row E
1. Walk ... Stop
2. Point to the floor ... Raise your arm
3. Put your arm down ... Turn around
4. Sit down ... Turn around on the floor
5. Get up ... Point to the floor

SECTION 1: CARTOON STRIPS

LESSON TWO

Row A
1. Get up ... Sit down
2. Raise your arm ... Walk
3. Stop ... Put your arm down
4. Point to the floor ... Walk
5. Stop ... Put your arms up

Row B
1. Put your arms down ... Turn around
2. Point to the floor ... Touch the floor
3. Sit down on the floor ... Get up
4. Turn around ... Raise your arms
5. Put your arms down ... Raise your arm

Row C
1. Put your arm down ... Turn around
2. Touch your head ... Touch your stomach
3. Touch the floor ... Walk
4. Stop ... Touch your stomach
5. Touch your head ... Touch the floor

Row D
1. Point to the floor ... Raise your arms
2. Put your arms down ... Turn around twice (one, two)
3. Touch your stomach twice ... Touch your head
4. Touch the floor ... Walk
5. Stop ... Turn around

Row E
1. Sit down ... Get up
2. Turn around ... Touch the chair
3. Touch your stomach ... Touch the floor
4. Point to the floor ... Point to the floor twice (one, two)
5. Point to the chair ... Touch the chair

SECTION 1: CARTOON STRIPS

LESSON THREE

Row A
1. Sit down ... Get up
2. Walk to the table ... Point to the table
3. Touch the table ... Sit down on the table
4. Get up ... Walk
5. Stop ... Put your arms up

Row B
1. Put your arms down ... Point to the floor
2. Point to your stomach ... Touch your stomach
3. Touch your head ... Point to your head
4. Raise your arm ... Raise your arms
5. Put your arms down ... Walk to the chair

Row C
1. Touch the chair ... Turn around
2. Sit down on the chair ... Get up
3. Touch the floor ... Point to the floor
4. Sit down on the floor ... Get up
5. Jump ... Jump again

Row D
1. Walk fast ... Stop
2. Walk slowly ... Stop
3. Walk to the table ... Sit down on the table
4. Touch the table with your head ... Walk
5. Stop ... Turn around

Row E
1. Walk to the door ... Open the door slowly
2. Close the door ... Open the door again
3. Close the door ... Touch the door
4. Point to the door ... Point to your head
5. Point to the floor ... Jump twice (1, 2)

SECTION 1: CARTOON STRIPS

LESSON FOUR

Row A
1. Turn around slowly ... Turn around fast
2. Walk ... Walk fast
3. Walk slowly ... Stop
4. Point to the floor twice (1, 2) ... Touch the floor
5. Sit down on the floor ... Get up

Row B
1. Raise your arm slowly ... Put your arm down fast
2. Point to the light ... Turn around slowly
3. Sit down slowly ... Get up fast
4. Raise your arms ... Put your arms down slowly
5. Walk fast ... Halt

Row C
1. Turn around fast ... Walk to the chair
2. Sit down on the chair slowly ... Get up slowly
3. Touch the chair fast ... Point to the chair twice (1, 2)
4. Walk to the table ... Point to the table slowly
5. Jump ... Jump again

Row D
1. Walk fast ... Run
2. Stop ... Walk to the table
3. Sit down on the table slowly ... Get up fast
4. Touch the table with your head ... Walk
5. Halt ... Turn around twice (1, 2)

Row E
1. Walk to the door ... Point to the door
2. Touch the door ... Open the door
3. Close the door ... Open the door
4. Close the door slowly ... Point to the floor
5. Point to your head ... Touch your stomach

SECTION 1: CARTOON STRIPS

LESSON FIVE

Row A
1. Jump ... Jump again
2. Walk ... Halt!
3. Point to the floor ... Touch the floor
4. Run to the table ... Sit on the table
5. Get up ... Walk to the chair

Row B
1. Touch the chair ... Point to the chair
2. Raise the chair ... Put the chair down
3. Walk ... Halt!
4. Walk slowly ... Run
5. Stop ... Walk slowly

Row C
1. Halt! ... Run to the door
2. Touch the door ... Point to the door
3. Open the door ... Close the door
4. Touch the door with your head .... Walk to the chair
5. Point to the chair ... Touch the chair

Row D
1. Sit down fast ... Stand up slowly
2. Walk ... Stop
3. Walk fast ... Halt!
4. March ... March slowly
5. Stop ... Touch your stomach

Row E
1. Point to the floor ... Point to your head
2. Touch your head ... Touch your head with your arm
3. Touch your arm ... Sit down fast
4 Get up ... Lift the chair
5. Put the chair down ... Go to the door

SECTION 1: CARTOON STRIPS

LESSON SIX

Row A
1. Go to the chalkboard ... Touch the chalkboard
2. Point to the chalkboard ... Raise your arm
3. Touch your head with your arm ... Touch the chair
4. Sit down on the chair ... Get up
5. Lift the chair slowly ... Put the chair on the floor

Row B
1. Walk slowly ... Halt!
2. Walk fast ... Stop
3. March slowly ... March fast
4. Stop ... Run to the chalkboard
5. Touch the chalkboard with your head ... Turn around fast

Row C
1. Go to the door ... Open the door
2. Shut the door ... Raise your arm slowly
3. Touch your hand ... Point to your hand
4. Turn around slowly ... Go to the table
5. Go to the chair ... Lift the chair

Row D
1. Walk to the table and pick up the chair ... Put the chair on top of the table
2. Turn around ... Walk
3. Halt! ... Return to the table with the chair on top
4. Lift the chair from the table ... Put the chair down
5. Sit down fast ... Sit down on the chair fast slowly

Row E
1. Point to the chair with both hands ... Touch the chair
2. Go to the table with the box on top... Touch the box
3. Pick up the box ... Carry the box to the door
4 Place the box on the floor in front of the door ... Return to your chair
5. Sit down on your chair slowly... Get up fast

SECTION 1: CARTOON STRIPS

LESSON SEVEN

Row A
1. Jump twice (1, 2) ... Jump twice again
2. Raise your arms ... Sit down on the floor
3. Turn around on the floor ... Get up
4. Turn on the light ... Turn off the light
5. Go to the door ... Pick up the box from the floor

Row B
1. Carry the box to the chair... Put the box on the chair
2. Raise your right arm ... Put your arm down
3. Raise your left arm ... Raise your arms
4. Put your right arm down ... Point to your right arm
5. Cut the paper in two ... Return to your chair

Row C
1. Pick up the box from the chair ... Take the box to the table
2. Place the box under the table ... Point to the table twice
3. Walk to the chalkboard ... Point to the chalkboard
4. Write your name on the board ... Erase your name
5. Write your last name on the board ... Erase your last name

Row D
1. Run to the door... Touch the door with both hands
2. Open the door ... Close the door slowly
3. March to the table ... Touch the box on top of the table
4. Point to the box ... Open the box
5. Close the box ... Pick up the box

Row E
1. Place the box on the floor ... Count with your fingers
2. Scratch your left ear ... Raise your right arm
3. Walk ... Stop
4 Put your arm down slowly ... Turn around fast
5. Point to your right hand ... Point to your left hand

SECTION 1: CARTOON STRIPS

LESSON EIGHT

Row   A
1. Turn around twice ... Turn around slowly
2. Touch the floor with your left hand... Point to the floor with your right hand
3. Walk fast to the board ... Point to the chalkboard with both hands
4. Write down your name on the board ... Write down your surname
5. Erase your name ... Erase your surname

Row   B
1. Write down on the board the professor's last name ... Write down your father's name
2. Draw a head on the board ... Draw a bigger head
3. Draw the eyes ... Erase the left eye
4. Erase everything ... Raise your arms
5. Put your arms down ... Go to the table

Row   C
1. Sit down under the table ... Push the table
2. Go to the table with the basket on top ... Pick up the basket with both hands
3. Put the basket on the floor ... Put your right foot inside the basket
4. Take your foot out of the basket ... Put your head inside the basket
5. Take out your head of the basket ... Touch the floor with your right hand

Row   D
1. Sit down on the floor ... Touch your shoes
2. Touch your right arm ... Get up
3. Go to the board ... Draw a hand
4. Erase the fingers ... Erase everything
5. Draw a bow ... Erase the box

Row   E
1. Draw a chair ... Erase the chair
2. Point to the light ... Raise your right arm
3. Roll up the paper ... Unroll the paper
4 Count with your fingers ... Turn around slowly
5. Push the chair ... Sit down on the chair

SECTION 1: CARTOON STRIPS

LESSON NINE

Row A
1. March to the chalkboard ... Touch the board
2. Draw the professor on the board ...   Erase the professor's nose
3. Erase the left eye ... Erase everything
4. Turn around twice ... Go to the chair
5. Point to the chair ... Lift the chair

Row B
1. Push the chair ... Touch your head
2. Point to your stomach ... Point to the light
3. Point to your nose ... Touch your nose
4. Point to the hand ... Point to the fingers
5. March forward ... Stop

Row C
1. Raise your right arm ... Walk
2. Stop ... Put your arm down
3. Run ... Stop
4. Roll in the paper ... Unroll the paper
5. Go to the table with the hat on top ... Put the hat on

Row D
1. Take off your hat ... Walk with the hat on your right hand
2. Place the hat on the chair ... Put the hat on the floor beneath the chair
3. Turn around ... Go to the table with the basket on top
4. Pick up the basket with your left hand ... Carry the basket to the table with the small box on top
5. Place the small box on the floor ... Pick the basket and put it on your head

Row E
1. Applaud the teacher ... Squat on the floor
2. Go to the board ... Draw a house
3. Draw a door to the house ... Draw two windows to the house
4 Erase the windows ... Erase the floor of the house
5. Erase the door ... Erase everything

SECTION 1: CARTOON STRIPS

LESSON TEN

Row A
1. Turn off the light ... Turn on the light
2. Close the door ... Open the door
3. Open your hand ... Close your hand
4. Close your eyes ... Open your right eye
5. Open your eyes ... Close your right eye

Row B
1. Go to the table with the box on top ... Take out the small box from the box
2. Place the small box to the right of the box ... Open the box
3. Point to the box ... Point to the small box
4. Go to the board ... Draw a table
5. Draw a small table to the left of the table ... Erase the small table

Row C
1. Erase the legs of the table ... Erase everything
2. Draw a house and small house ... Erase the roof of the house with both hands
3. Turn around twice slowly ... March forward
4. Halt! ... Put both hands on your head
5. Turn around ... Raise your arms fast

Row D
1. Go to the door ... Point to the door
2. Touch the door ... Cut the paper in two
3. Count with your fingers ... Sit down
4. Go to the table ... Push the table
5. Sit down under the table ... Lift the table with your head

Row E
1. Turn around ... Sit down on the floor
2. Lie down on the floor ... Get up
3. Sit down ... Stand up
4 Sit down ... Get up
5. Sit down on the table ... Get up

SECTION 1: CARTOON STRIPS

LESSON ELEVEN

Row A
1. Put your hat on ... Take off your hat
2. Turn on the light ... Turn off the light
3. Go to the television set ... Turn on the TV
4. Turn off the TV ... Touch the chair
5. Touch the TV ... Point to the floor

Row B
1. Point to your nose ... Point to your head
2. Point to your right eye ... Cover your left eye with your right hand
3. Pull down your hair ... Raise your arms
4. Put your arms down ... Turn around
5. Run ... Stop

Row A
1. Carry the basket with the left hand ... Carry the basket with the right hand
2. Go to the TV with the basket ... Place the basket on the TV
3. Raise your left arm ... Raise both arms
4. Raise the left hand and put down your right arm ... Count with your fingers
5. March forward ... Halt!

Row D
1. Cross your arms ... Extend out your arms
2. Put your arms down ... Cross your legs
3. Raise your right leg ... Jump
4. Go to the door ... Touch the door
5. March slowly ... Stop

Row E
1. Sit down ... Sand up slowly
2. Go to the board ... Draw a bed on the board
3. Erase the legs of the bed ... Draw a church
4. Erase the cross of the church ... Erase everything
5. Return to your chair ... Sit down on the chair

SECTION 1: CARTOON STRIPS

LESSON TWELVE

Row A
1. Run very fast ... Stop
2. March to the TV ... Sit down in front of the TV
3. Turn on the TV... Turn off the light
4. Turn off the TV ... Turn on the light
5. Point to the light ... Point to the chair

Row B
1. Count with your fingers ... Raise your arms
2. Applaud the teacher ... Touch the floor with the left hand
3. Touch your stomach ... Turn around
4. Raise your arm ... Walk
5. Stop ... Put your arm down

Row C
1. Go to the bed ... Sit down on the bed
2. Lie down on the bed ... Go to the table
3. Sit down on the table ... Get up
4. Touch the floor with your left hand ... Sit down under the table
5. Push the chair ... Lift the chair up

Row D
1. Put the chair on top of the table... Lift the chair from the table
2. Take the chair to the board ... Write your name on the board with your left hand
3. Erase your name with the right hand ... Point to the door
4. Pick up the box from the floor ... Carry the box to the chair
5. Take the box to the table ... Open the Box

Row E
1. Place the box beneath the table ... Return to your chair
2. Squat on the floor ... Kneel on the floor
3. Get up ... Turn around
4 Point to your right eye ... Scratch your left ear
5. Raise your arms ... Put your arms down

SECTION 2 : CHAINING

CHAIN ONE

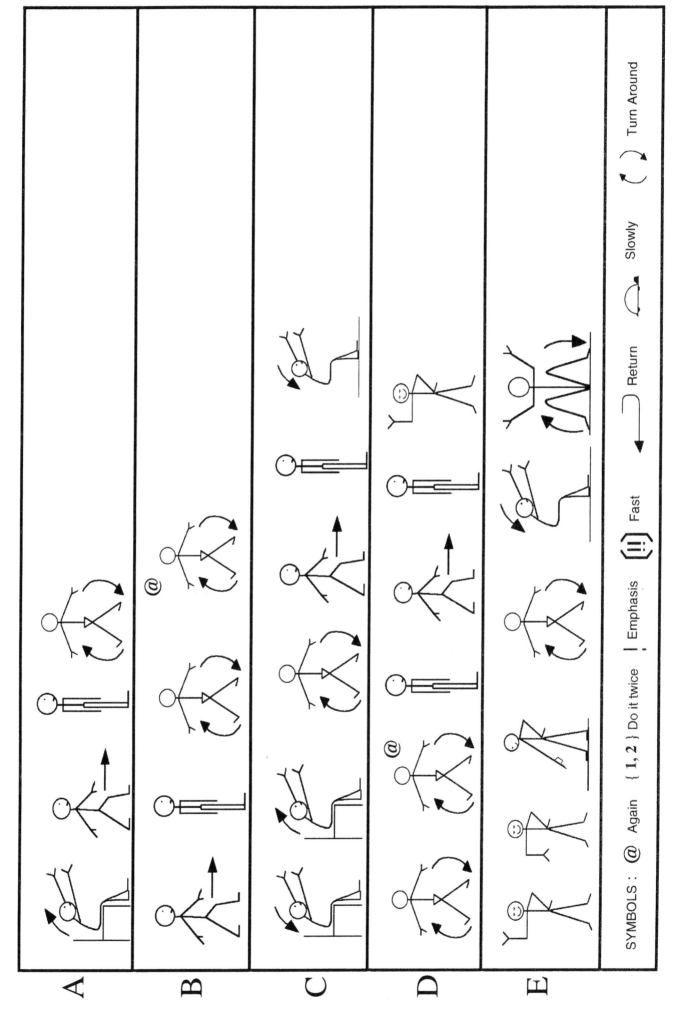

SYMBOLS : @ Again { 1, 2 } Do it twice ! Emphasis [!] Fast ⤵ Return ⌒ Slowly ( ) Turn Around

SECTION 2: CHAINING

CHAIN TWO

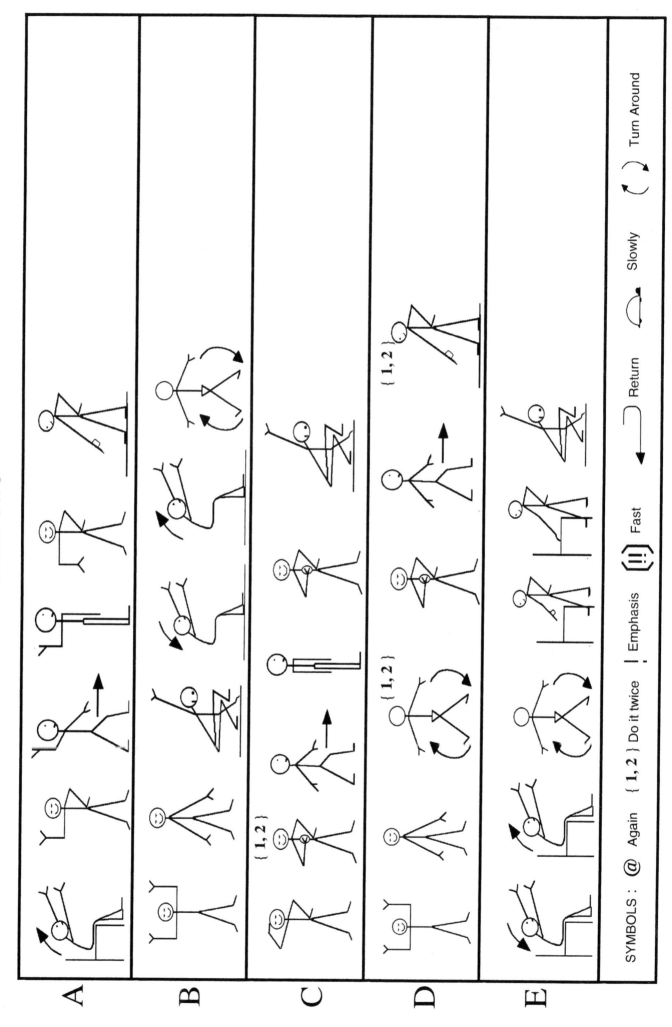

SYMBOLS: @ Again { 1, 2 } Do it twice ! Emphasis (!!!) Fast ⟶ Return ⌒ Slowly ( ) Turn Around

SECTION 2 : CHAINING

CHAIN THREE

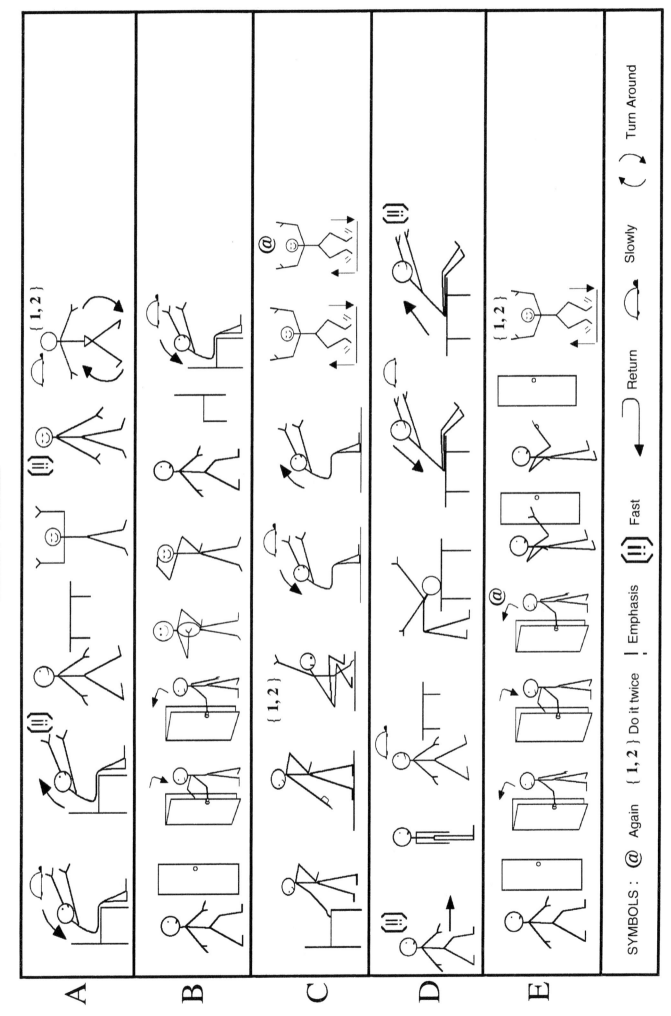

SYMBOLS : @ Again   { 1, 2 } Do it twice   ! Emphasis   [≡] Fast   ⌒ Slowly   ↰ Return   ⟲ Turn Around

SECTION 2 : CHAINING

CHAIN FOUR

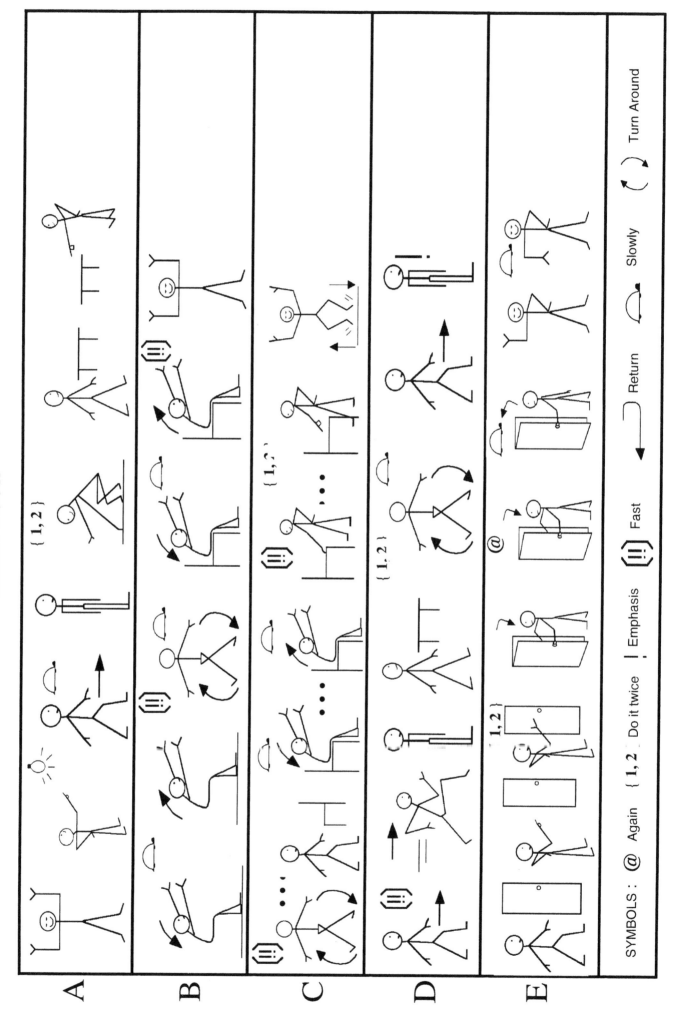

SYMBOLS :   @ Again   { 1, 2 } Do it twice   ! Emphasis   ⟨⟩ Turn Around

   @ Again   ⌒ Slowly   ‖ Return

   | Emphasis   ⬡ Fast

SECTION 2: CHAINING

CHAIN FIVE

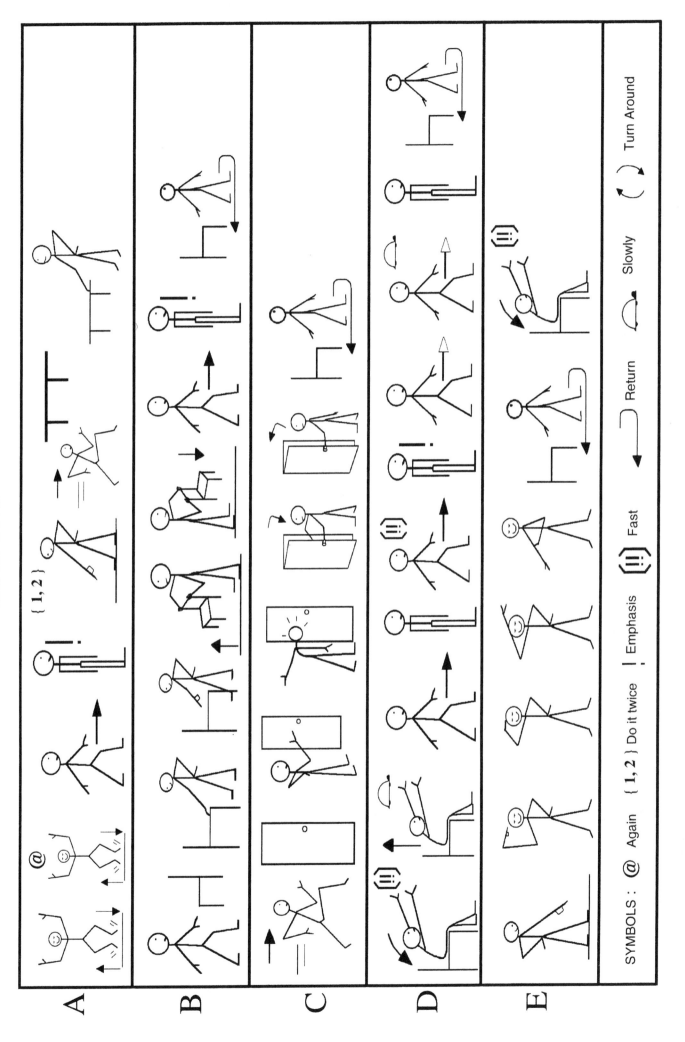

SYMBOLS : @ Again { 1, 2 } Do it twice ! Emphasis {≡} Fast ⌒ Slowly ⟲ Turn Around ⌐ Return

SECTION 2 : CHAINING

CHAIN SIX

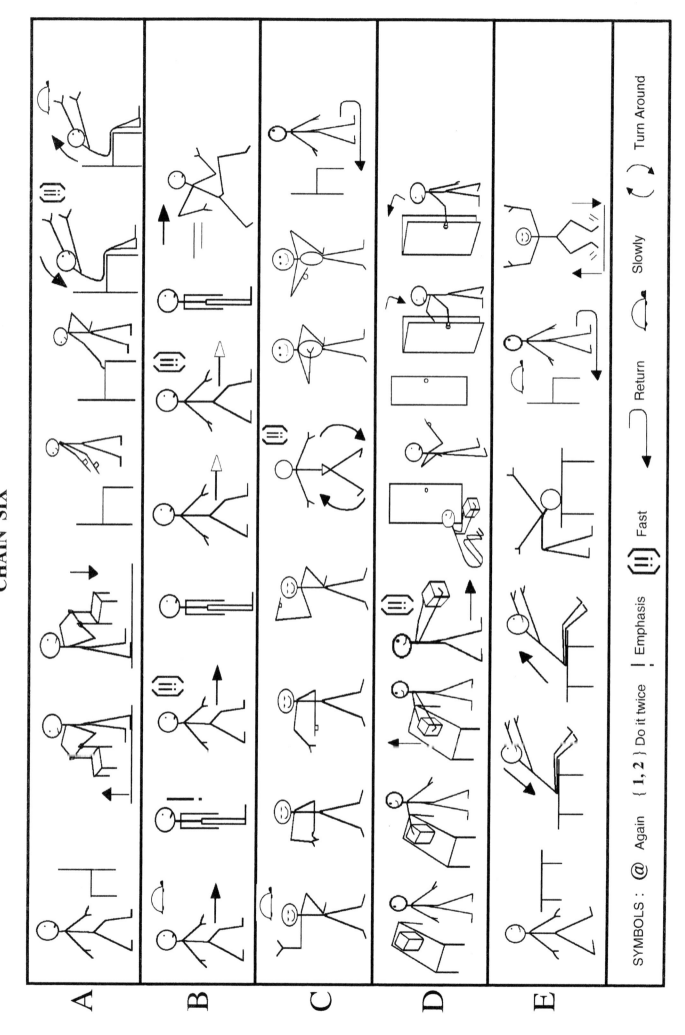

SYMBOLS : @ Again   { **1, 2** } Do it twice   ! Emphasis   Fast   Return   Slowly   Turn Around

SECTION 2 : CHAINING

CHAIN SEVEN

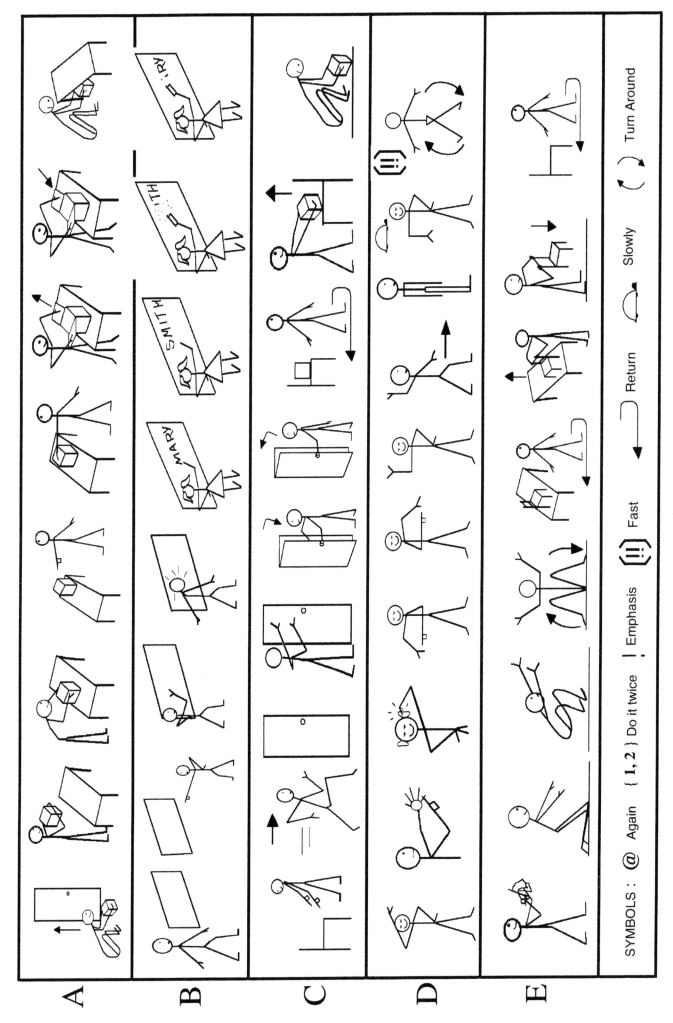

SYMBOLS : @ Again { 1, 2 } Do it twice | Emphasis [ii] Fast ⌒ Slowly ( ) Turn Around ⊐ Return

SECTION 2 : CHAINING

CHAIN EIGHT

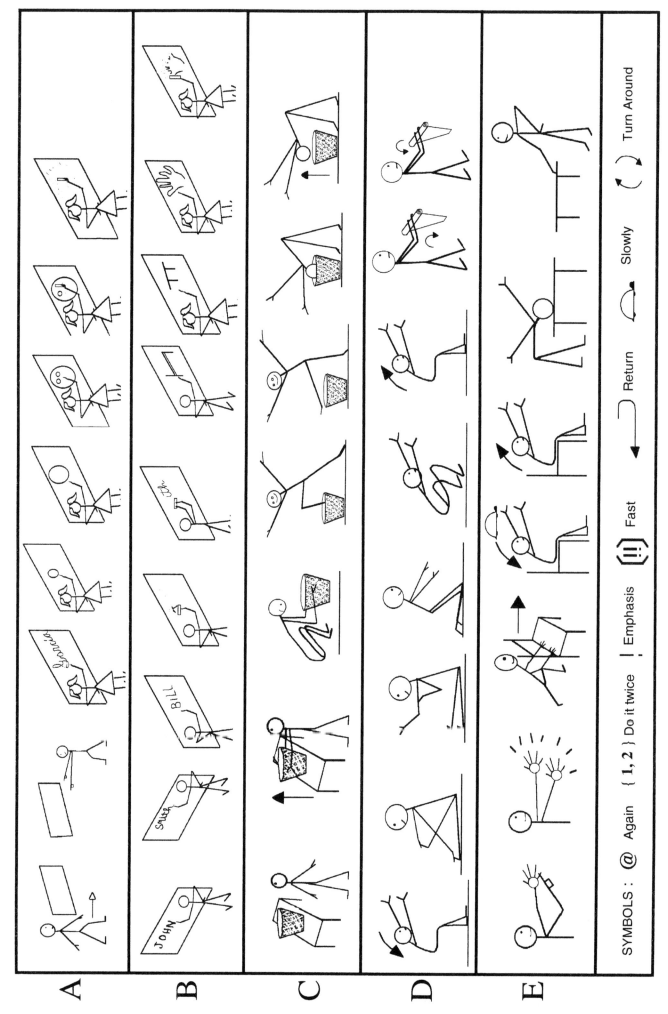

SYMBOLS : @ Again { 1, 2 } Do it twice ! Emphasis [!!] Fast ⌒ Return ⌢ Slowly ( ) Turn Around

SECTION 2 : CHAINING

CHAIN NINE

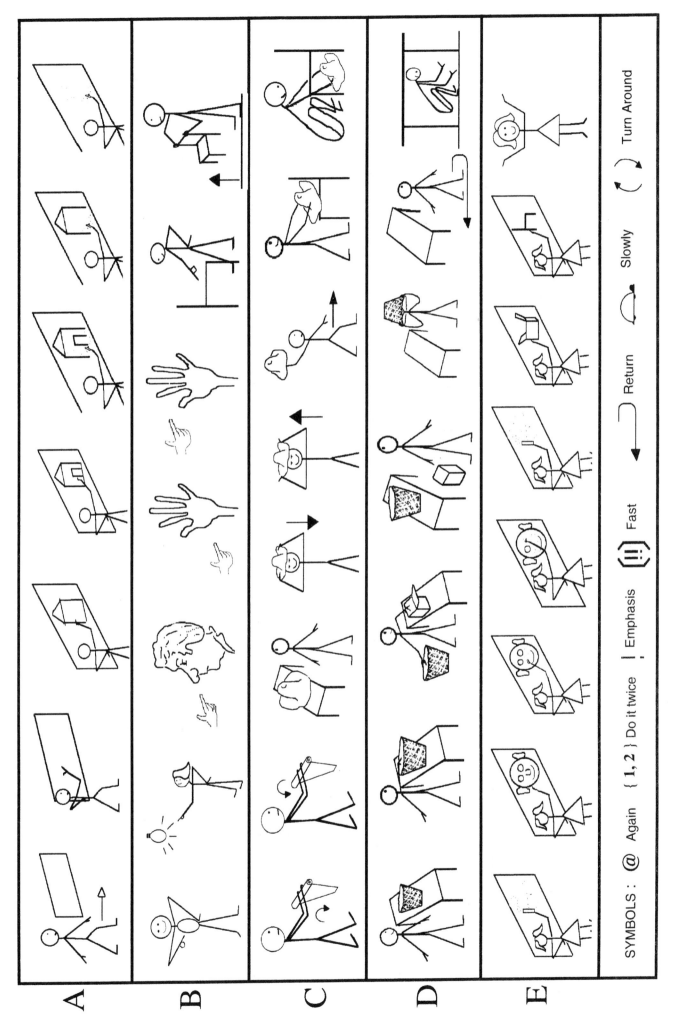

SYMBOLS : @ Again { 1, 2 } Do it twice ! Emphasis [!|!] Fast ⌐ Return ⌒ Slowly ↻ Turn Around

SECTION 2: CHAINING

CHAIN TEN

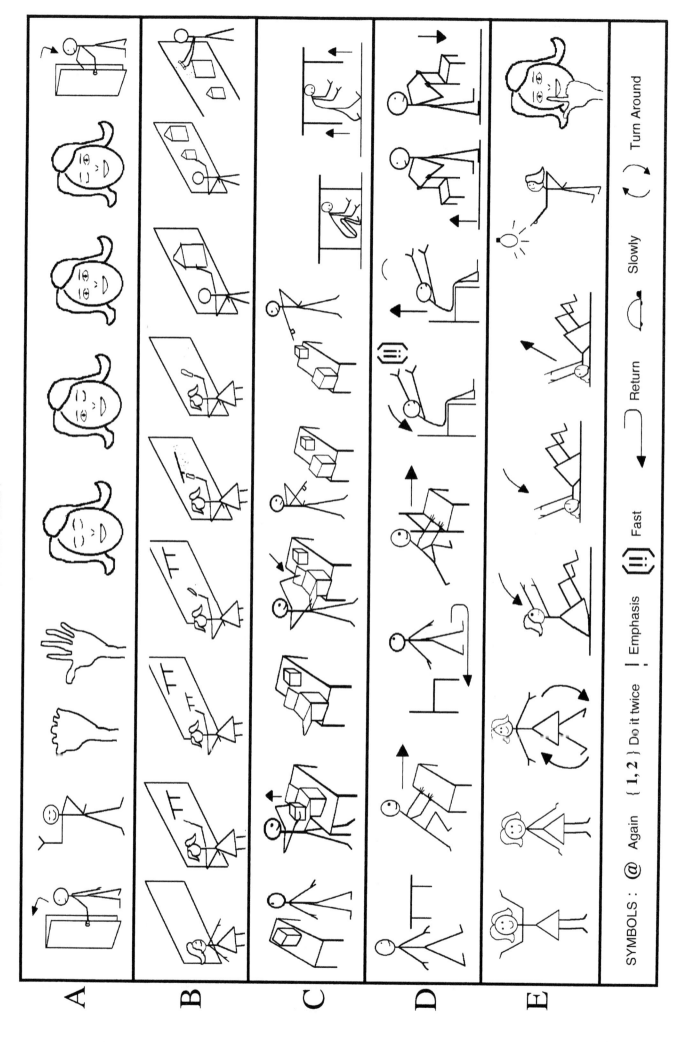

SYMBOLS: @ Again   { 1, 2 } Do it twice | Emphasis   (!!!) Fast   Slowly   Return   Turn Around

SECTION 2: CHAINING

CHAIN ELEVEN

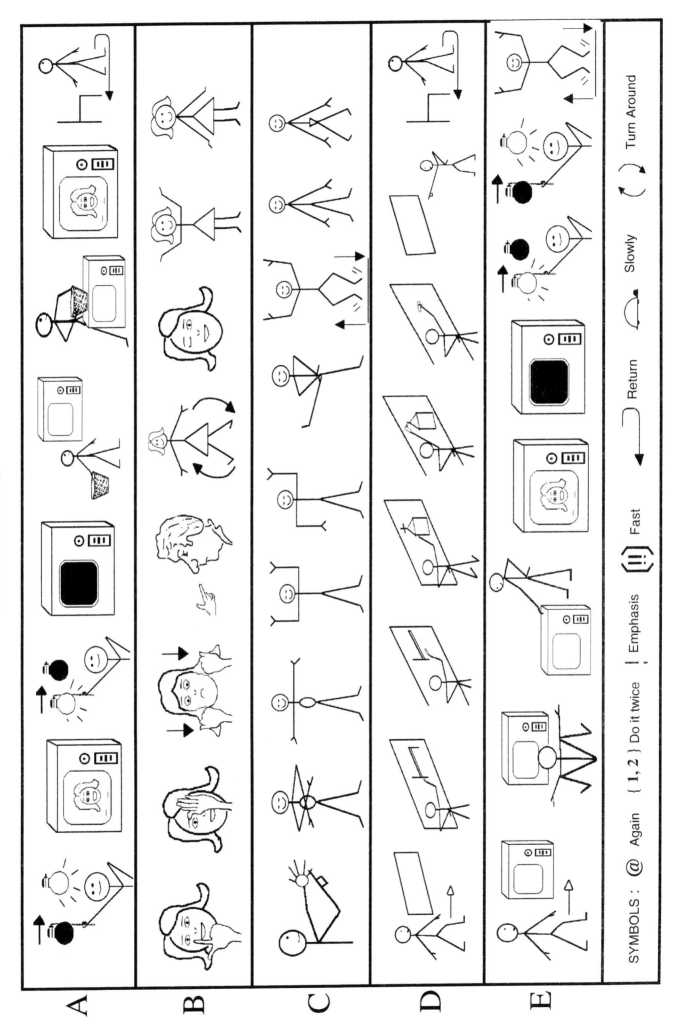

SYMBOLS : @ Again { 1, 2 } Do it twice | Emphasis [:] Fast ⌐ Return ⌒ Slowly ⟲ Turn Around

SECTION 2 : CHAINING

CHAIN TWELVE

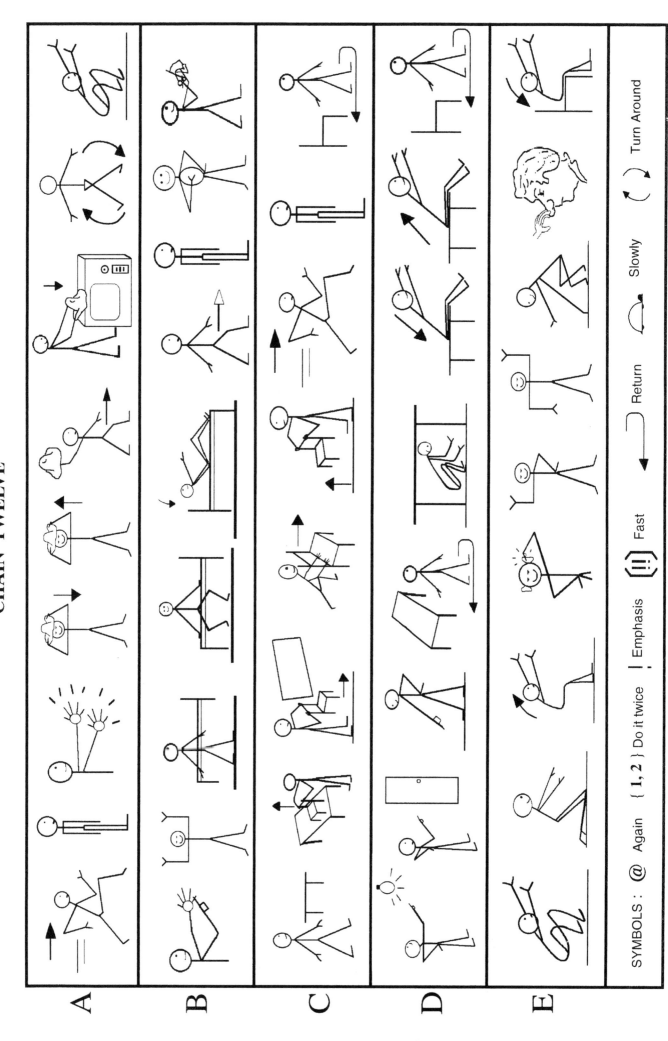

SYMBOLS : @ Again   { 1, 2 } Do it twice | Emphasis   [!!] Fast   ⌢ Return   ⌢ Slowly   ↻ Turn Around

SECTION 2: CHAINING

CHAIN ONE

Row A   Get up, Walk, Stop, Turn around.

Row B   Walk, Stop, Turn around, Turn around again.

Row C   Sit down, Get up, Turn Around, Walk, Stop, Sit down on the floor.

Row D   Turn around, Turn around again, Stop, Walk, Raise your arm.

Row E   Raise your arm, Put your arm down, Point to the floor, Turn around.
Sit down on the floor, Turn around on the floor.

CHAIN TWO

Row A   Get up, Raise your arm, Walk, Stop, Put your arm down, Point to the floor.

Row B   Raise your arms, Put your arms down, Touch the floor, Sit down on the floor,
Get up from the floor, Turn around.

Row C   Touch your head, Touch your stomach twice, Walk, Stop, Touch your stomach
again, Touch the floor

Row D   Raise your arms, Put your arms down, Turn around twice, touch your stomach,
Walk, Point to the floor twice.

Row E   Sit down, Get up, Turn around, Point to the chair. Touch the chair, Touch the
floor.

CHAIN THREE

Row A   Sit down slowly, Get up fast, Go to the table, Raise your arms.
Put your arms down fast, Turn around twice slowly.

Row B   Go to the door, Open the door, Close the door, Touch your stomach,
Touch your head, Go to the chair, Sit down slowly.

Row C   Touch the chair, Point to the floor, Touch the floor, Sit down on the floor,
Get up from the floor, Jump, Jump again.

Row D   Walk fast, Stop, Go to the table slowly, Touch the table with your head,
Sit down on the table slowly, Get up from the table fast.

Row E   Go to the door, Close the door, Open the door, Close the door again
Point to the door, Jump twice.

SECTION 2: CHAINING

CHAIN FOUR

Row A   Raise your arms, Point to the light, Walk slowly, Stop, Touch the floor,
Go to the table, Point to the table.

Row B   Sit down on the floor, Get up fast, Turn around slowly, Sit down slowly,
Get up fast, Raise your arms.

Row C   Turn around fast, Go to the chair, Sit down slowly, Get up slowly
Touch the chair fast, Point to the chair twice, Jump.

Row D   Walk fast, Run, Stop, Go to the table, Turn around twice, Walk, Halt!

Row E   Go to the door, Point to the door, Touch the door twice, Open the door,
Open the door again.

CHAIN FIVE

Row A   Jump, Jump again, Walk, Halt!, Point to the floor twice, Run to the table.
Touch the table.

Row B   Go to the chair, Touch the chair, Point to the chair, Lift the chair up,
Put the chair down, Walk, Halt!, Return to your chair.

Row C   Run to the door, Touch the door, Touch the door with your head, Open the door
Close the door, Return to your chair.

Row D   Sit down on the chair fast, Stand up slowly, Walk, Stop, Walk fast, Halt!,
Go froward, Go forward slowly, Stop, Return to your chair.

Row E   Point to the floor, Point to your head, Touch your head with your arm, Touch
your right arm, Return to your chair, Sit down fast.

CHAIN SIX

Row A   Go to the chair, Lift the chair, Put the chair down on the floor,
Point to the chair with the two hands, Touch the chair, Sit down fast,
Get up slowly.

Row B   Walk slowly, Halt!, Walk fast, Stop, March, March fast, Stop, Run.

Row C   Raise your arm slowly, Touch your hand, Point to your hand, Point to your
head, Turn around fast, Touch your stomach, Point to your stomach,
Return to your chair.

Row D   Go to the table with the box on top, Touch the box,   Pick up the box
Carry the box to the door, Place the box in front of the door, Point to the door,
Open the door, Close the door.

Row E   Go to the table, Sit on the table, Get up from the table, Touch the table with
your head, Return to your chair slowly, Jump.

SECTION 2: CHAINING

CHAIN SEVEN

Row A Pick up the box from the floor, Carry the box to the table, Put the box on the table, Point to the box, Touch the box, Open the box, Place the box under the table on the floor.

Row B Go to the board, Point to the board, Touch the board, Touch the board with your head, Write your name on the board, Write your last name Erase your last name, Erase your name.

Row C Point to the chair with both hands, Run to the door, Touch the door with both hands, Open the door, Close the door, Return to your chair, Pick up the box from the chair, Place the box on the floor.

Row D Touch your head with your arm, Count with your fingers, Scratch your left ear, Point to your left hand, Point to your right hand, Raise your arm, Walk, Stop, Put your arm down slowly, Turn around fast.

Row E Cut the paper in two, Kneel on the floor, Squat on the floor, Turn around on the floor, Return to the table with the chair on top, Lift the chair, Place the chair on the floor, return to your chair.

CHAIN EIGHT

Row A Go to the chalkboard, Point to the board with both hands, Write on the board the instructor's last name, Draw a head on the board, Draw a bigger head, Draw two eyes, Erase the left eye, Erase everything.

Row B Write your name on the board with your left hand, Write your surname, Write your father's name, Erase your father's name, Erase your last name with both hands, Draw a bed on the board, Draw a table, Draw a hand, Erase the fingers of the hand.

Row C Go to the table with the basket on top, Pick up the basket with both hands, Place the basket on the floor, Put your right foot inside the basket, Take your foot out of the basket, Put your head inside the basket, Take your head out of the basket.

Row D Sit down on the floor, touch your shoes, Touch your right arm, Kneel on the floor, Squat on the floor, Get up from the floor, Roll the paper in, Unroll the paper.

Row E Count with your fingers, Applaud the Instructor, Push the chair, Sit down slowly, Get up, Touch the table with your head, Touch the table.

SECTION 2: CHAINING

CHAIN NINE

Row A   March to the board, Touch the board, Draw a house, Draw a door to the house, Erase the floor of the house, Erase the door, Erase everything.

Row B   Point to the stomach, Point to the light, Point to the nose, Point to the hand, Point to the fingers, Point to the chair, Lift the chair.

Row C   Roll the paper in, Unroll the paper, Go to the table with the hat on top, Pick up the hat and put it on, Take off the hat, Raise the right hand and carry the hat in your hand, Put the hat on the chair, Place the hat under the chair.

Row D   Go to the table with basket on, Pick up the basket with your left hand, Go to the table with the box on, Pick up the small box with the left hand and switch the basket to the right hand, Place the small box on the floor and place the basket on the table, Put the basket on your head, Return to the table, Sit under the table.

Row E   Erase the board, Draw the professor on the board, Erase the nose, Erase the left eye, Erase everything, Draw a box, Draw a chair, Raise your arms, Place the chair on the floor, return to your chair.

CHAIN TEN

Row A   Close the door, Raise your right hand, Close your hand, Open your hand, Close your eyes, Open your right eye, Open your eyes, Close your right eye, Open the door.

Row B   Go to the blackboard, Draw a table, Draw a small table to the left of the table, Erase the small table, Erase the legs of the table, Erase everything, Draw a house, Draw a small house to the left of the house, Erase the roof of the house.

Row C   Go to the table with the box on top, Take the small box out of the Box, Place the small box on the table to the right of the box, Point to the box, Point to the little box, Sit down under the table, Stand up and lift the table on your head.

Row D   Go to the table, Push the table, Return to the chair, Push the chair, Sit down on the chair fast, Stand up slowly, Lift the chair, Put the chair on the floor.

Row E   Raise your arms, Put your arms down, Turn around, Sit on the floor, Lie down on the floor, Point to the light, Point to your right eye.

SECTION 2: CHAINING

CHAIN ELEVEN

Row A Turn on the light, Turn off the TV, Turn off the light, Turn off the TV, Carry the basket to the TV, Put the basket on top of the TV, Turn on the TV, Return to your chair.

Row B Point to your right eye, Cover your left eye with your right hand, Pull down your hair, Point to the nose, Turn around, Close your right eye, Raise your arms, Put your arms down.

Row C Count with your fingers, Cross your arms, Extend your arms out, Raise your arms, Put down your right arm, Raise your right leg, Jump, Put your arms down, Cross your legs.

Row D March to the board, Draw a bed on the board, Erase the legs of the bed, Draw a church on the board, Erase the cross of the church, Erase everything, Return to your chair.

Row E March to the TV set, Sit down on the floor in front of the TV, Touch the TV, Turn on the TV, Turn off the TV, Turn off the light, Turn on the light, Jump.

CHAIN TWELVE

Row A Run, Stop, Give a hand to the teacher, Put your hat on, Take off your hat, Carry the hat to the TV set, Put the hat on top of the TV, Turn around, Squat on the floor.

Row B Count with your fingers, Put your arms up, Walk to your bed, Sit on the bed, Lie down on the bed, March, Stop, Touch your stomach, Cut the paper in halves.

Row C Go to the table, Pick the chair from the top of the table, Take the chair to chalkboard, Push the chair, Lift the chair, Run, Stop, Return to your chair.

Row D Point to the light, Point to the door, Point to the floor, Return to the table, Sit on the floor beneath the table, Sit on the table, Get up from the table, Return to your chair.

Row E Squat on the floor, Kneel on the floor, Get up, Scratch your left ear, Raise your right arm, Raise your left arm and put down your right hand, Touch the floor with your left hand, Touch the nose, Sit down.

SECTION 3: PICTURE DESCRIPTIONS

EXERCISE 1   Write something that goes with each picture. Write as many details as you can. It is ok to write something funny. Be entertaining!

Example:

Put your arms up. I want your money! Why are you smiling? Why are you not wearing any clothes?

1. _____

2. _____

3. _____

4. _____

5. _____

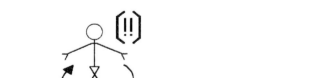

6. _____

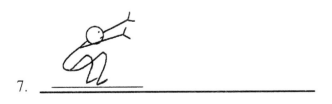

7. _____

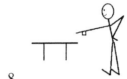

8. _____

9. _____

10. _____

11. _____

12. _____

13 _____

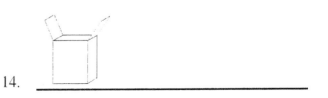

14. _____

SECTION 3: PICTURE DESCRIPTIONS

EXERCISE 2   Write something that goes with each picture. Write as many details as you can. It is ok to write something funny. Be entertaining!

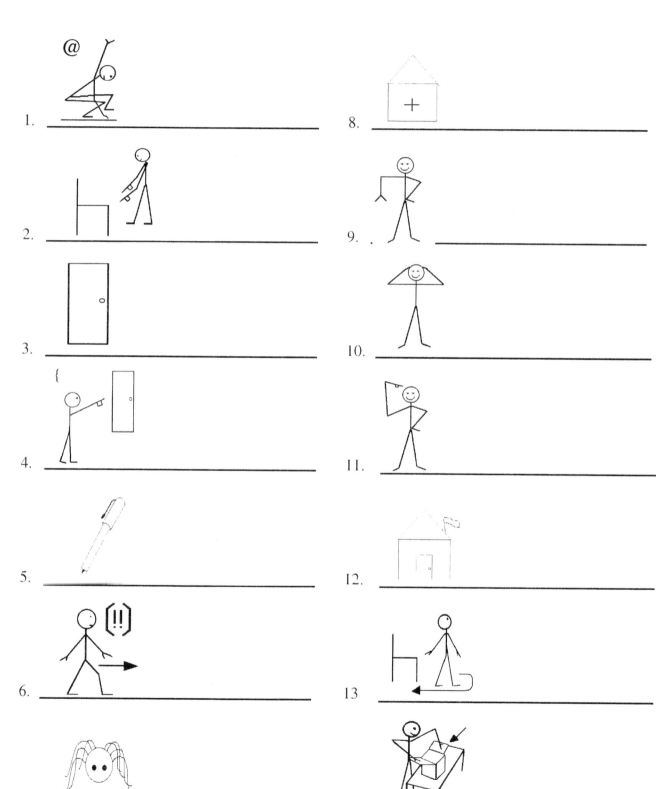

1. _____

2. _____

3. _____

4. _____

5. _____

6. _____

7. _____

8. _____

9. _____

10. _____

11. _____

12. _____

13. _____

14. _____

SECTION 3: PICTURE DESCRIPTIONS

EXERCISE 3   Write something that goes with each picture. Write as many details as you can. It is ok to write something funny. Be entertaining!

1. _____

2. _____

3. _____

4. _____

5. _____

6. _____

7. _____

8. _____

9. _____

10. _____

11. _____

12. _____

13 _____

1⁴ _____

SECTION 3: PICTURE DESCRIPTIONS

EXERCISE 4   Write something that goes with each picture. Write as many details as you can. It is ok to write something funny. Be entertaining!

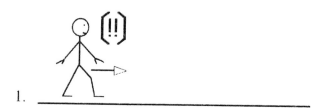
1. _____

2. _____

3. _____

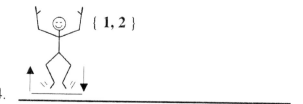
4. _____

5. _____

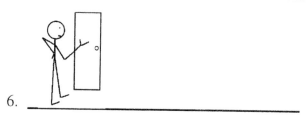
6. _____

5
7. _____

8. _____

9. _____

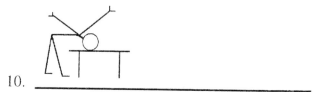
10. _____

11. _____

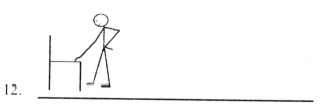
12. _____

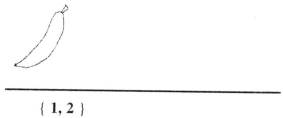
13. _____

14. _____

SECTION 3: PICTURE DESCRIPTIONS

EXERCISE 5 Write something that goes with each picture. Write as many details as you can. It is ok to write something funny. Be entertaining!

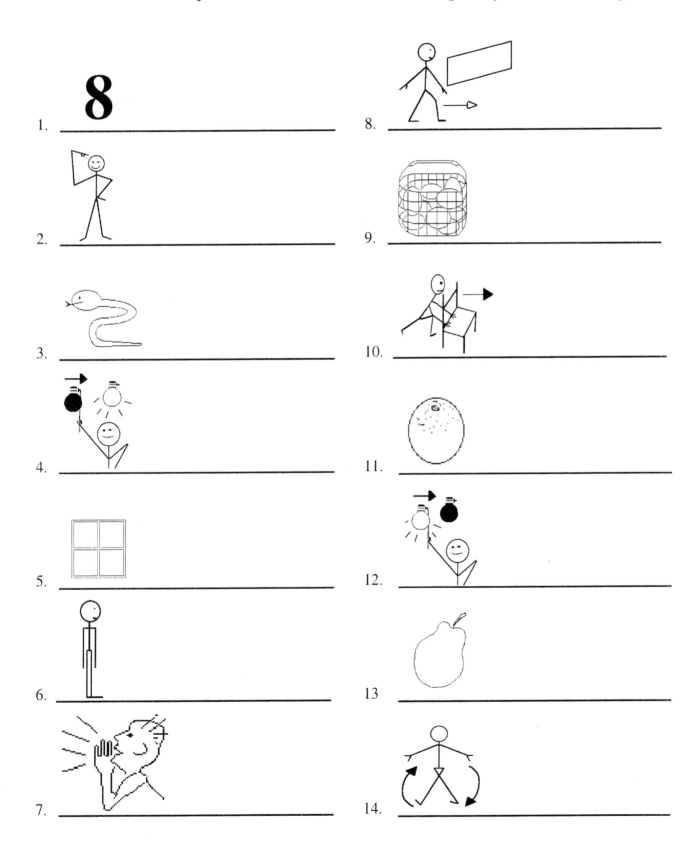

1. _____

2. _____

3. _____

4. _____

5. _____

6. _____

7. _____

8. _____

9. _____

10. _____

11. _____

12. _____

13 _____

14. _____

SECTION 3: PICTURE DESCRIPTIONS

EXERCISE 6   Write something that goes with each picture. Write as many details as you can. It is ok to write something funny. Be entertaining!

1. _____

2. _____

3. _____

4. _____

5. _____

6. _____

7. _____

8. _____

9. _____

10. _____

11. _____

12. _____

13. _____

14. _____

SECTION 3: PICTURE DESCRIPTIONS

EXERCISE 7   Write something that goes with each picture. Write as many details as you can. It is ok to write something funny. Be entertaining!

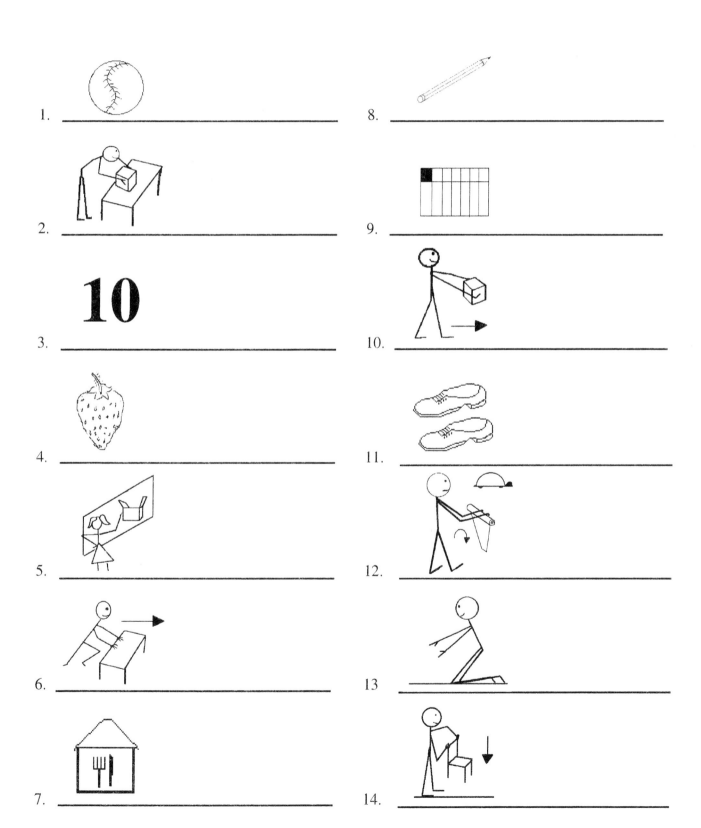

1. _____

2. _____

3. _____

4. _____

5. _____

6. _____

7. _____

8. _____

9. _____

10. _____

11. _____

12. _____

13. _____

14. _____

SECTION 3: PICTURE DESCRIPTIONS

EXERCISE 8   Write something that goes with each picture. Write as many details as you can. It is ok to write something funny. Be entertaining!

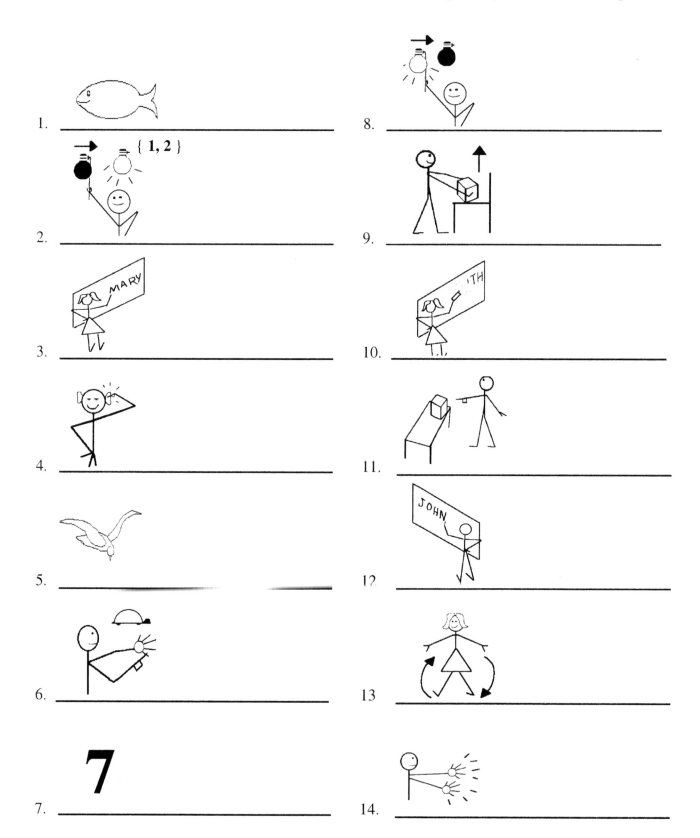

1. _____

2. _____

3. _____

4. _____

5. _____

6. _____

7.

8. _____

9. _____

10. _____

11. _____

12. _____

13. _____

14. _____

SECTION 3: PICTURE DESCRIPTIONS

EXERCISE 9   Write something that goes with each picture. Write as many details as you can. It is ok to write something funny. Be entertaining!

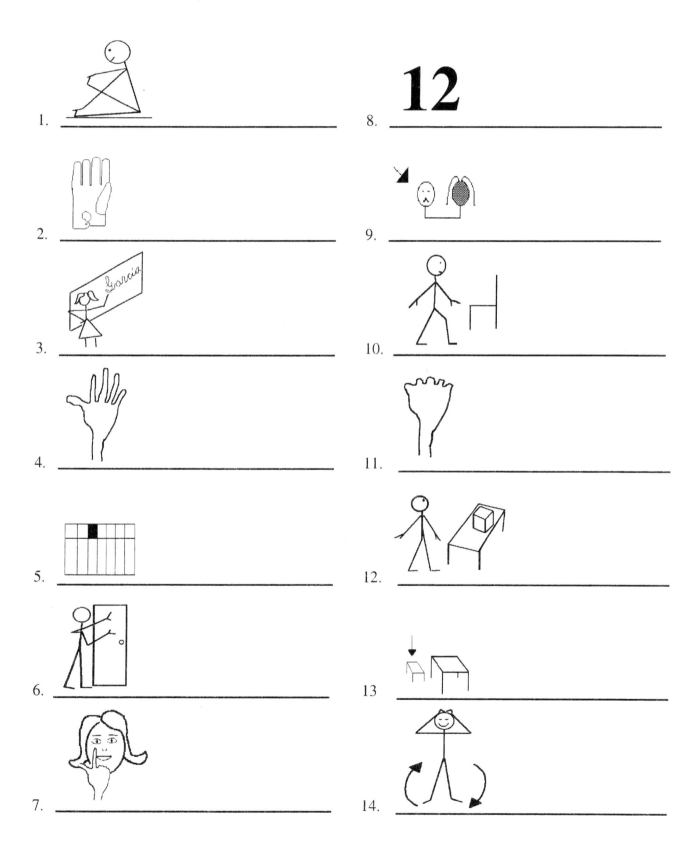

1. _____

2. _____

3. _____

4. _____

5. _____

6. _____

7. _____

8. _____

9. _____

10. _____

11. _____

12. _____

13 _____

14. _____

SECTION 3: PICTURE DESCRIPTIONS

EXERCISE 10   Write something that goes with each picture. Write as many details as you can. It is ok to write something funny. Be entertaining!

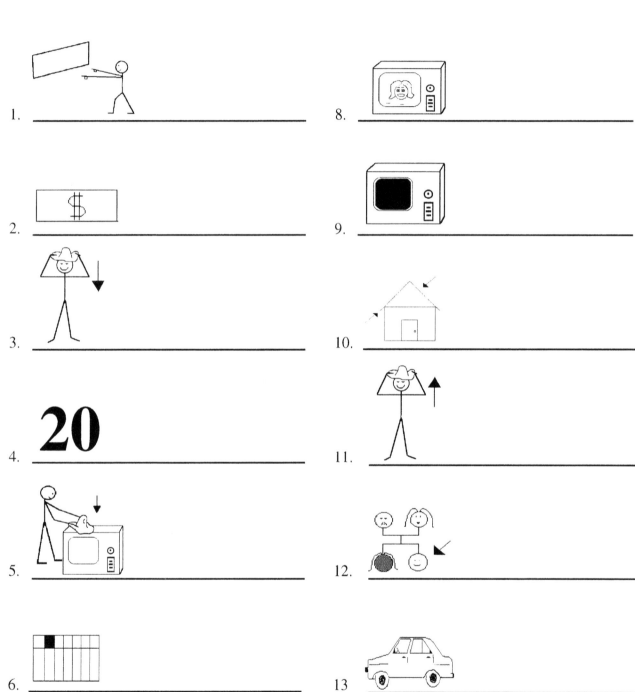

1. _____

2. _____

3. _____

4. _____

5. _____

6. _____

7. _____

8. _____

9. _____

10. _____

11. _____

12. _____

13 _____

14. _____

SECTION 3: PICTURE DESCRIPTIONS

EXERCISE 11   Write something that goes with each picture. Write as many details as you can. It is ok to write something funny. Be entertaining!

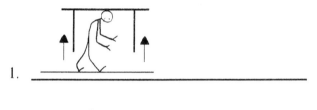

1. _____

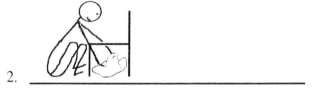

2. _____

11

3. _____

4. _____

5. _____

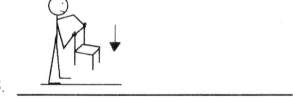

6. _____

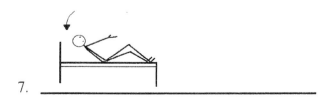

7. _____

8. _____

9. _____

10. _____

11. _____

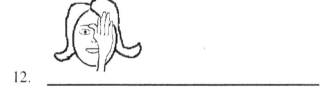

12. _____

13 _____

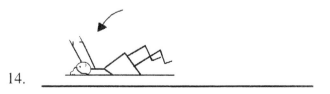

14. _____

SECTION 3: PICTURE DESCRIPTIONS

EXERCISE 12   Write something that goes with each picture. Write as many details as you can. It is ok to write something funny. Be entertaining!

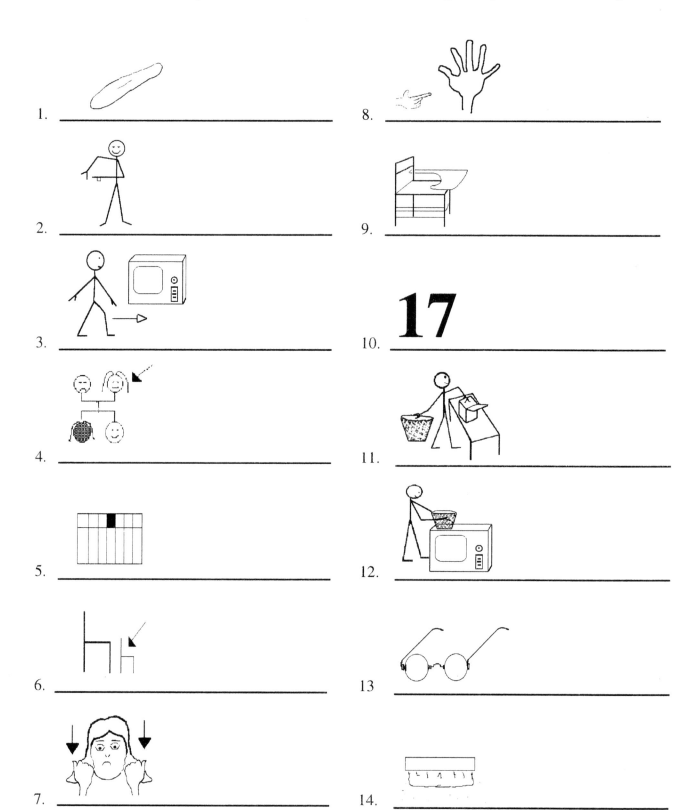

1. _____

2. _____

3. _____

4. _____

5. _____

6. _____

7. _____

8. _____

9. _____

10. _____

11. _____

12. _____

13. _____

14. _____

SECTION 3: PICTURE DESCRIPTIONS

EXERCISE 13   Write something that goes with each picture. Write as many details as you can. It is ok to write something funny. Be entertaining!

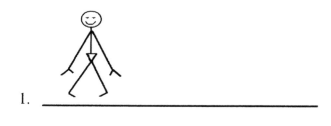

1. _____

2. _____

3. _____

4. _____

5. _____

6. _____

7. _____

8. _____

18

9. _____

10. _____

11. _____

12. _____

13. _____

14. _____

SECTION 3: PICTURE DESCRIPTIONS

EXERCISE 14   Write something that goes with each picture. Write as many details as you can. It is ok to write something funny. Be entertaining!

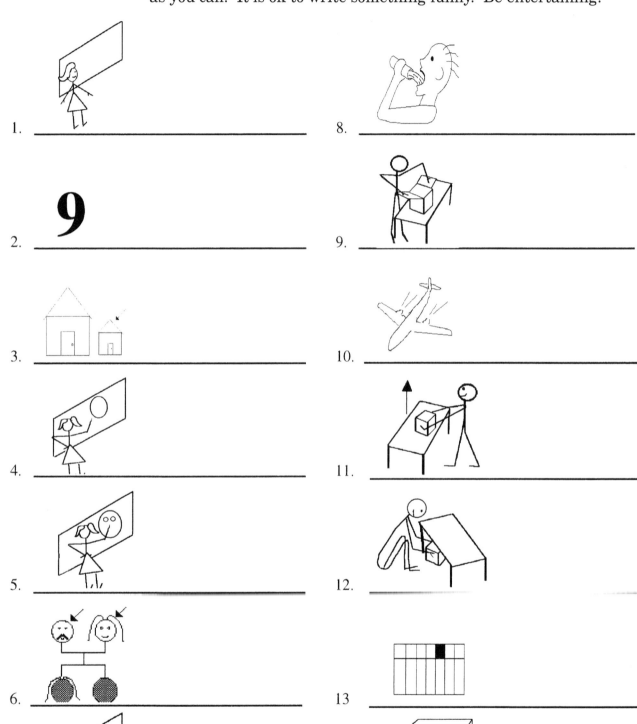

1. _____

2. _____

3. _____

4. _____

5. _____

6. _____

7. _____

8. _____

9. _____

10. _____

11. _____

12. _____

13 _____

14. _____

SECTION 3: PICTURE DESCRIPTIONS

EXERCISE 15 Write something that goes with each picture. Write as many details as you can. It is ok to write something funny. Be entertaining!

1. _____

2. _____

3. _____

4. _____

5. _____

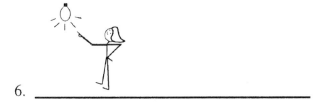

6. _____

7. _____

8. _____

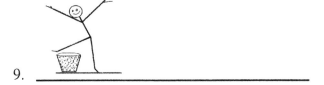

9. _____

10. _____

11. _____

12. _____

13. _____

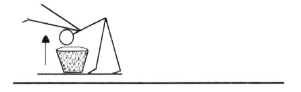

14. _____

SECTION 3: PICTURE DESCRIPTIONS

EXERCISE 16   Write something that goes with each picture. Write as many details as you can. It is ok to write something funny. Be entertaining!

1. _____

2. _____

3. _____

4. _____

5. _____

6. _____

7. _____

8. _____

9. _____

10. _____

11. _____

12. _____

13. _____

14. _____

SECTION 3: PICTURE DESCRIPTIONS

EXERCISE 17   Write something that goes with each picture. Write as many details as you can. It is ok to write something funny. Be entertaining!

1. _____

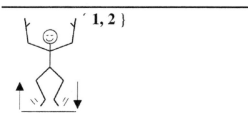

2. _____

3. _____

4. _____

5. _____

6. _____

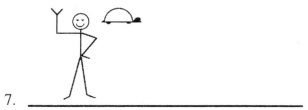

7. _____

8. _____

9. _____

10. _____

11. _____

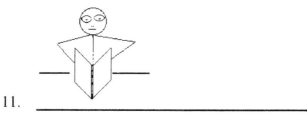

12. _____

13 _____

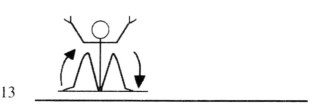

14. _____

SECTION 3: PICTURE DESCRIPTIONS

EXERCISE 18 Write something that goes with each picture. Write as many details as you can. It is ok to write something funny. Be entertaining!

1. 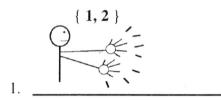 _____

2. 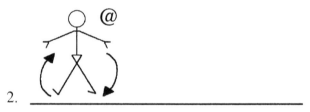 _____

3. 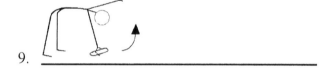 _____

4. 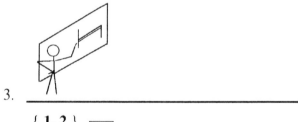 _____

5. **14** _____

6.  _____

7. **70** _____

8. **30** _____

9.  _____

10.  _____

11.  _____

12. 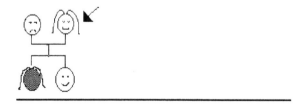 _____

13.  _____

14.  _____

SECTION 3: PICTURE DESCRIPTIONS

EXERCISE 19   Write something that goes with each picture. Write as many details as you can. It is ok to write something funny. Be entertaining!

{ 1, 2 }

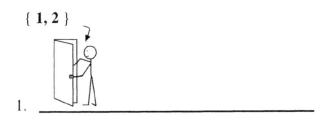

1. _____

2. _____

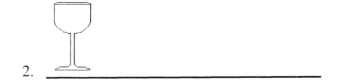

3. _____

4. _____

5. _____

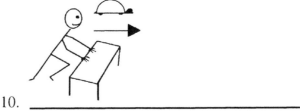

6. _____

7. _____

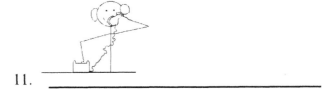

8. _____

9. _____

10. _____

11. _____

12. _____

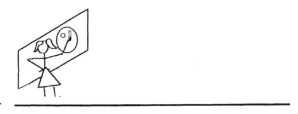

13. _____

14. _____

SECTION 3: PICTURE DESCRIPTIONS

EXERCISE 20   Write something that goes with each picture. Write as many details as you can. It is ok to write something funny. Be entertaining!

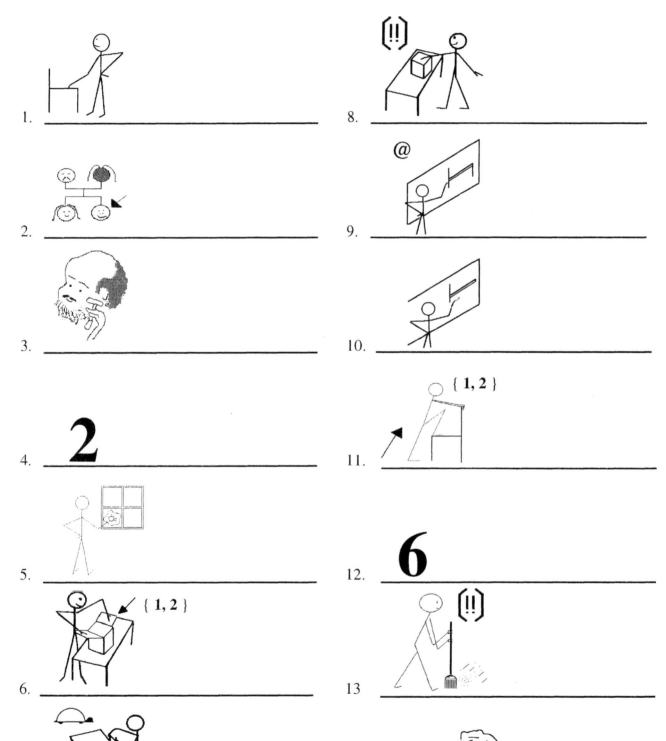

1. _____

2. _____

3. _____

4. _____

5. _____

6. _____

7. _____

8. _____

9. _____

10. _____

11. _____

12. _____

13. _____

14. _____

Order online: **tpr-world.com**

TPR PRODUCTS

Books • Games
Student Kits
Teacher Kits
Audio Cassettes
Video Demonstrations

Manufactured in the United States of America

Order directly from the publisher using your
VISA, MASTERCARD, or DISCOVER CARD
WE SHIP ASAP TO ANYWHERE IN THE WORLD!

Sky Oaks Productions, Inc.

Since 1973
P.O. Box 1102
Los Gatos, CA 95031 USA

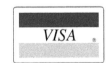

Phone: (408) 395-7600
Fax: (408) 395-8440
tprworld@aol.com

 For fast service,
order online:

tpr-world.com

Introduction
by the Originator of TPR, Dr. James J. Asher

Dear Colleague,

If you are new to TPR, start with a solid understanding by reading my book, **Learning Another Language Through Actions** and Ramiro Garcia's **Instructor's Notebook: How to apply TPR for best results**.

To ensure success, pretest a few lessons before you enter your classroom. Try the lessons out with your children, your friends or your neighbors. In doing this, you

(a) become convinced that TPR actually works,

(b) build self-confidence in the approach, and

(c) smooth out your delivery.

For Students of All Ages, including Adults

Use TPR for new vocabulary and grammar, to help your students immediately understand the target language in chunks rather than word-by-word. This instant success is absolutely thrilling for students. You will hear them say to each other, "Wow! I actually understand what the instructor is saying."

After a "silent period" of about three weeks listening to you and following your directions in the target language (without translation), your students will be ready to talk, read and write. In our books, Ramiro and I will guide you step-by-step along the way.

Be sure to look through our online catalog at **www.tpr-world.com**. It's loaded with activities that will keep your students excited day after day as they move towards fluency in the target language.

Best wishes for continued success,

James J Asher

Students who drop out of school are not stupid.

They are smart enough to know that "school" is not meeting their needs. And you know what? The kids are right: The traditional school does not work for 1/3 to 1/2 of our students.

From the San Jose Mercury News, April 10, 2009:

"Kids dropping out of San Jose schools in just one year may go on to commit 534 violent crimes and suffer 200 million in lost wages over their lifetimes... according to a new study released Thursday... Statewide, for every three students who graduated high school in 2006-7, one dropped out..."

Let's turn it around. Let's make school relevant for <u>all</u> our kids:

The Super School of the 21st Century
by James J. Asher, Ph.D.

Table of Contents

Discoveries by Ordinary People that Changed the World

News Flash!

by James J. Asher

Commentary by Albert Einstein

A fresh look at science, and technology in 25 exciting true stories such as:

- How two brothers, who own a bicycle shop in Ohio, build a bicycle that can fly.
- How penicillin is discovered when wind blows in some dirt from an open window.
- How an American student discovers the secret of DNA, and becomes the youngest person ever to win a Nobel Prize. His discovery transformed everyone's life in the 21st Century; yet amazingly, Harvard University tried to ban his personal story from publication.
- How a junior member of an Italian university discovers a simple equation that predicts the distance objects fall in space in seconds. A stunning discovery made even more remarkable when all he had to work with was a crude measure of time: water dripping from a bottle.
- How a fifteen year old boy discovers patterns of dots that enable blind people to read and write.
- How an uneducated janitor in London discovers simple patterns of electricity to enable giant turbines to move millions of gallons of water.
- How a young Englishman read about the principle of falling objects in space, adds one small detail, and discovers the jewel of mathematics, calculus, to predict how planets move around the sun. When you see that tiny detail, you will say, "Wow! So that is what calculus is all about!"

Order#	Title
2	Discoveries by Ordinary People that Changed the World

New!

I just completed a 263 page memoir about growing up in the 1930s, 40s, and 50s. I think you will have so much fun reading it you will want to start your own memoir today.

Comments from readers:

…"I started reading the book in bed and could not put it down."

…"I want several copies as gifts for friends."

…"I did not want the book to end."

…"The characters were so real, I felt I could reach out and touch them."

…"I remember reading **Catcher in the Rye** as a kid. This coming of age book is even better."

…"This is going to be a blockbuster of a motion picture."

After you read *Growing Up in Norman Rockwell's America*, please send me your comments!

James J. Asher

tprworld@aol.com

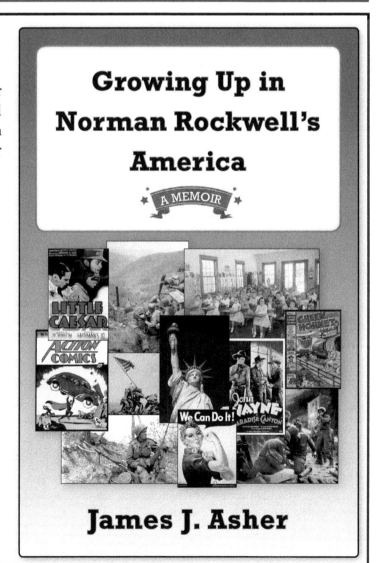

Order#	Title	
5	Growing Up in Norman Rockwell's America	263 pages

Captured for the first time on DVD!

Dr. James J. Asher
Originator of TPR

The Northeastern Conference of FL/ESL instructors
Invited presentation by **Dr. James J. Asher**

New!

Exciting 30 minute TPR demonstration in Arabic and Spanish followed by a lively Q&A session.
Narrated in English

Includes:

- How to stretch single words into hundreds of interesting sentences in any language.
- Your students will understand sentences, they have never heard before in the target language. This is the secret of fluency.
- Why it is <u>not</u> wise to tell your students, "Listen and repeat after me!"
- How to deal with adjectives.
- How to deal with grammar.

- How to make the transition from understanding to speaking, reading and writing.
- How to deal with abstractions.
- How to graduate your students with three or more languages.
- How to put your school on the map. Get ready for the Greyhound bus stopping at your school with teachers from around the world who want to take a look at your program.

Order Number: 104-DVD

Strategy for Second Language Learning

Your students can enjoy the thrill of achieving basic fluency in one or more languages if they remain in the program long enough. The problem is they "give up" too soon.

A solution
You will see adults of all ages from 17 to 60 understanding everything the instructor is saying in German. Within five minutes of the first class meeting, the faces of the adults reveal that they are convinced they can actually learn German.

After only a few weeks, students are ready to reverse roles and give directions in German. You will be entertained with their directions in German that have the instructor standing on a table and sitting in a corner. You will be impressed because you are witnessing the students actually thinking in the target language.

The grand climax
You will see the smooth transition from understanding German to speaking, reading, and writing within eight weeks. Time lapse photography will show you in 60 seconds, one student's progress through the entire course from zero understanding of German to conversational skill.

Show this video to your students
Instructors worldwide in all languages use this video to prepare their students to participate in the exciting TPR experience.

A bonus
As a bonus, we will include a copy of the original research article published in the *Modern Language Journal* that documents the significant achievement of the adults you will see in the video.

Strategy for Second Language Learning *(Order # 407-DVD)*

Produced by James J. Asher • DVD • Color • 19 minutes • Narrated in English

Dear Colleague:

Language instructors often say to me, "I tried the TPR lessons in your book and my students responded with great enthusiasm, but what can the students do **at their seats**?"

Here are effective TPR activities that students can perform **at their seats**. Each student has a kit in full color, such as the interior of a kitchen. Then you say in the target language, "Put the man in front of the sink." With your kit displayed so that it is clearly visible to the students, you place the man in the kitchen of your kit and your students follow by performing the same action in their kits.

As items are internalized, you can gradually discontinue the modeling. Eventually, you will utter a direction and the students will quickly respond without being shown what to do.

Each figure in the **TPR Student Kits** will stick to any location on the playboard **without glue**. Just press and the figure is on. It can be peeled off instantly and placed in a different location over and over.

You can create fresh sentences that give students practice in understanding hundreds of useful vocabulary items and grammatical structures. Also, students quickly acquire "function" words such as **up, down, on, off, under, over, next to, in front of,** and **behind**.

To guide you step-by-step I have written ten complete lessons for each kit (giving you about 200 commands for each kit design), and those lessons are now available in your choice of **English, Spanish, French, German,** or **Dutch**. The kits can be used with **children or adults** who are learning **any language** including **ESL** and the **sign language of the deaf**.

About the TPR Teacher Kits

Use the **transparencies** with an overhead projector to flash a playboard on a large screen. Your students **listen** to you utter a direction in the target language, **watch** you perform the action on the large screen, and then follow by performing the same action in their **Student Kits.**

Best wishes for continued success,

James J Asher

P.S. My sister and I recently tried one of the Student Kits with a native speaker of Arabic giving directions. We were both surprised at how much vocabulary and grammar we picked up in only a few minutes of play.

Try this with any language you would like to acquire from Turkish to Chinese to Hebrew. It is simple, fast-moving, and it works!

Back By Popular Demand!

For every 5 Kits (Student or Teacher) in <u>any</u> assortment,
select an additional kit of your choice as our <u>Free</u> <u>Gift</u> to you!

James J. Asher's TPR STUDENT KITS™

More than 300,000 Kits now being used in FL-ESL classes throughout the world!!

	ENGLISH Order Number	SPANISH Order Number	FRENCH Order Number	GERMAN Order Number	DUTCH Order Number
Airport ©	4E	4S	4F	4G	4D
Beach ©	12E	12S	12F	12G	12D
Classroom ©	10E	10S	10F	10G	10D
Garden ©	17E	17S	17F	17G	17D
Department Store ©	13E	13S	13F	13G	13D
Farm ©	60E	60S	60F	60G	60D
Gas Station ©	5E	5S	5F	5G	5D
Now Available ➥ Home ©	1E	1S	1F	1G	1D
Hospital ©	21E	21S	21F	21G	21D
Kitchen ©	2E	2S	2F	2G	2D
Main Street ©	15E	15S	15F	15G	15D
New ➥ Office ©	6E	6S	6F	6G	n/a

*...ludes high tech business machines such as computers,
cell phones, and even satellite communications!)*

	ENGLISH	SPANISH	FRENCH	GERMAN	DUTCH
Picnic ©	16E	16S	16F	16G	16D
Playground ©	20E	20S	20F	20G	20D
Restaurant ©	40E	40S	40F	40G	40D
Supermarket ©	11E	11S	11F	11G	11D
Town ©	3E	3S	3F	3G	3D
United States Map ©	22E	22S	22F	n/a	n/a
New ➥ European Map ©	23E	23S	23F	23G	23D

(Recently updated to include the Middle East!)

	ENGLISH	SPANISH	FRENCH	GERMAN	DUTCH
4-KITS-IN-ONE: Community, School, Work, Leisure ©	50E	50S	50F	50G	50D

Calendar © (limited supply) 31   (In English)

TPR Student Kit Stories ©Uses vocabulary from the Student Kits.   Order Number 33

TPR TEACHER KITS™
Transparencies for an <u>Overhead</u> <u>Projector</u>

	ENGLISH Order Number	SPANISH Order Number	FRENCH Order Number	GERMAN Order Number	DUTCH Order Number
Airport ©	4ET	4ST	4FT	4GT	4DT
Beach ©	12ET	12ST	12FT	12GT	12DT
Classroom ©	10ET	10ST	10FT	10GT	10DT
Garden ©	17ET	17ST	17FT	17GT	17DT
Dept. Store ©	13ET	13ST	13FT	13GT	13DT
Farm ©	60ET	60ST	60FT	60GT	60DT
Now Available ➥ Home ©	1ET	1ST	1FT	1GT	1DT
Hospital ©	21ET	21ST	21FT	21GT	21DT
Kitchen ©	2ET	2ST	2FT	2GT	2DT
Main Street ©	15ET	15ST	15FT	15GT	15DT
New ➥ Office ©	6ET	6ST	6FT	6GT	n/a
Picnic ©	16ET	16ST	16FT	16GT	16DT
Playground ©	20ET	20ST	20FT	20GT	20DT
Supermarket ©	11ET	11ST	11FT	11GT	11DT
Town ©	3ET	3ST	3FT	3GT	3DT
U.S. Map ©	22ET	22ST	22FT	n/a	n/a
New ➥ European Map ©	23ET	23ST	23FT	23GT	23DT

Children Learning Another Language: An Innovative Approach

Produced by James J. Asher
DVD • Color • 26 minutes • Narrated in English

> If you are searching for other ways that motivate young people to acquire other languages, don't miss this demonstration with students in kindergarten through the 6th grade. The exciting ideas you will see can be applied in your classroom for any grade level and for any language including English as a second language.

You will see young people...

✓ enjoying immediate understanding of everything the instructor is saying in Spanish or French.

✓ excited to be in the class day after day.

✓ spontaneously making the transition from understanding to speaking, reading, and writing.

✓ rapidly assimilating the target languages in chunks rather than word by word.

Be sure to show this video to your students

Use the video to prepare your students for the wonderful experience they are about to enjoy with TPR. The keen motivation and genuine achievement of these students will inspire parents, teachers and administrators at all levels.

A bonus

As a special bonus for you, we will include a complimentary copy of the original research published in *Child Development* that documents the extraordinary results you will see.

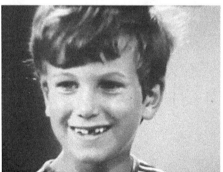

**Children Learning Another Language:
An innovative approach**

(Order # 435-DVD)

Order online: **www.tpr-world.com**

Order online: **tpr-world.com**

Demonstration of a New Strategy in Language Learning

Produced by James J. Asher
DVD • Black & White • 15 minutes • Narrated in English

This classic demonstration shows the complexity of spoken Japanese that American students can understand in only 20 minutes of TPR instruction. The Office of Naval Research was so impressed with this demonstration they awarded Dr. James J. Asher $50,000 to continue his ground-breaking research with the Total Physical Response, now known worldwide as TPR.

Shirou directs Hal Keely Jr. in Japanese to throw the toy car to him.

Retention after one year

You will be excited to witness the retention of the Japanese after one year. It is almost one-hundred percent.

Show this video to your students

Instructors worldwide in all languages use this video to prepare their students to participate in the exciting TPR experience.

A bonus

As a bonus, we will include a copy of the original research article published in the the *International Review of Applied Linguistics* that documents the significant achievement in Japanese of students like those you will see in the video.

Demonstration of a New Strategy in Language Learning
(Order # 408-DVD)
Order online: **www.tpr-world.com**

A powerful new tool for you, along with TPR and TPR Storytelling

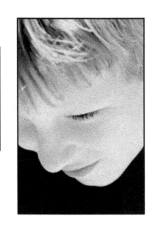

> ## Extra added attraction:
> ## Dr. James J. Asher explains what Tan-Gau is all about.

DVD • Black & White • 30 minutes • Narrated in English
Copyright 2009
Sky Oaks Productions, Inc.

"Live" Demonstration of Tan-Gau

✓ In your very first meeting with your students, you experience immediate success.

✓ Every student is comfortable.

✓ Students have great fun deciphering what Raymond is saying in French.

✓ Every student understands what is happening. No one is ever left behind.

Something extra

In this extraordinary demonstration, the instructor, Raymond, speaking to the students in an alien language, allows the students to respond in their native language. This means that students are completely at ease and receptive to what Raymond is saying in French. Watch the expressions on the faces of these young students.

Remarkable results after five years in Canadian schools!

Middle of the first year
Most students are speaking French.
End of the second year
All students are conversing in French.

A bonus

The new tool that you have never seen before works for all languages and all ages, including adults.

"Live" Demonstration of Tan-Gau!

(Order # 9-DVD)

Order online: **www.tpr-world.com**

TPR Storytelling

by

Todd McKay

**Outstanding Classroom Instructor
recently named to
Who's Who Among America's Teachers**

✔ Pre-tested in the classroom for 8 years to guarantee success for your students.

✔ Easy to follow, step-by-step guidance each day for three school years - one year at a time.

✔ Todd shows you how to switch from activity to activity to keep the novelty alive for your students day after day.

✔ Evidence shows the approach works: Students in storytelling class outperformed students in the traditional ALM class.

✔ Each story comes illustrated with snazzy cartoons that appeal to students of all ages.

✔ There is continuity to the story line because the stories revolve around one family.

✔ Complete with tests to assess comprehension, speaking, reading and writing.

✔ Yes, cultural topics are included.

✔ Yes, stories include most of the content you will find in traditional textbooks including vocabulary and grammar.

✔ Yes, included is a brief refresher of classic TPR, by the originator—
Dr. James J. Asher.

✔ Yes, games are included.

✔ Yes, your students will have the long-term retention you expect from TPR instructions.

✔ Yes, Todd includes his e-mail address to answer your questions if you get stuck along the way.

✔ Yes, you can order a video demonstration showing you step-by-step how to apply every feature in the Teacher's Guidebook.

Order Number	Title
400	Student Book - Year 1 **English**
401	Student Book - Year 2 **English**
402	Student Book - Year 3 **English**
410	Student Book - Year 1 **Spanish**
411	Student Book - Year 2 **Spanish**
412	Student Book - Year 3 **Spanish**
420	Student Book - Year 1 **French**
421	Student Book - Year 2 **French**
422	Student Book - Year 3 **French**
430	Complete Testing Packet for **English** Listening, Reading, Speaking, and Writing
431	Complete Testing Packet for **Spanish** Listening, Reading, Speaking, and Writing
432	Complete Testing Packet for **French** Listening, Reading, Speaking, and Writing
440	Teacher's Guidebook for **English**
441	Teacher's Guidebook for **Spanish**
442	Teacher's Guidebook for **French**
450	Transparencies for All Languages - Year 1
451	Transparencies for All Languages - Year 2
452	Transparencies for All Languages - Year 3
460	TPR Storytelling Video *Shows every step in the Teacher's Guidebook.*

450, 451 } Applies to Level 1, 2, 3

Sky Oaks Productions, Inc.
**P.O. Box 1102 • Los Gatos, CA, USA 95031
Phone: (408) 395-7600 • Fax: (408) 395-8440
e-mail: tprworld@aol.com
www.tpr—world.com**

California r( )ut notice.

Outside USA: for S&H add 30% (minimum: $13.95)
**Use your VISA, MasterCard, or Discover Card to order from anywhere in the world!
WE SHIP ASAP!**

Exciting new products from Todd McKay!
TPR Index Cards
(Easy-to-handle 4x5 cards)

1. Index cards tell you exactly what to say, lesson by lesson.
2. 60 Cards with vocabulary from First Year textbooks.
3. When your students internalize this vocabulary, they're ready for a smooth transition to stories.
4. No need to fumble through a book.
5. No need to make up your own lessons.
6. Quick! Easy to use! Classroom-tested for success!
7. Works for students of all ages, including adults!

470	TPR Index Cards for **English**
471	TPR Index Cards for **Spanish**
472	TPR Index Cards for **French**
473	TPR Index Cards for **German**

TRIPLE EXPANDED 4TH EDITION!

BEST-SELLER!!

For 20 years, Ramiro Garcia has successfully applied the **Total Physical Response** in his high school and adult language classes.

Four NEW Chapters in the **Triple Expanded 4th Edition** (288 pages):

- **Speaking, Reading, and Writing**
- **How to Create Your Own TPR Lessons.**

More than **200 TPR scenarios** for **beginning** and **advanced students.**

- **TPR Games** for **all age groups.**
- **TPR Testing** for **all skills** including **oral proficiency.**

In this illustrated book, Ramiro shares the tips and tricks that he has discovered in using TPR with hundreds of students. No matter what language you teach, including **ESL** and the **sign language of the deaf,** you will enjoy this insightful and humorous book.

Instructor's Notebook:
How to Apply TPR
For Best Results
By
RAMIRO GARCIA
Recipient of the
OUTSTANDING TEACHER AWARD

Order #	Title:	Recommendation:
225	**Instructor's Notebook:** How to Apply TPR for Best Results	**All Languages and All Ages**
224	**Instructor's Notebook:** TPR Homework Exercises	**Begin. & Interm. Students of All Ages**
	Ramiro's brand-new companion book to the Instructor's Notebook!	**All Languages**

The Graphics Book

For Students of <u>All</u> Ages
by **Ramiro Garcia**
Recipient of the Most Remembered Teacher Award

Dear Colleague,

You recall that I introduced graphics in the **Instructor's Notebook: How To Apply TPR For Best Results.** Hundreds of teachers tried the *graphics* with their students in many different languages including ESL and were excited to discover that **students of all ages** thoroughly enjoyed working with the material.

Your students understand a huge chunk of the target language because you used **TPR.** Now, with my new *graphics* book, you can follow up with *300 drawings* on tear-out strips and sheets that help your students *zoom ahead* with **more vocabulary, grammar, talking, reading, and writing** in the target language. In this book, you will receive **step-by-step guidance** in how to apply the *graphics* effectively with **children and adults** acquiring <u>any</u> **language, including ESL.**

As an **extra bonus,** you will discover how to use the *graphics* to **test the achievement of your students** in comprehension, speaking, reading, and writing. In fact, I provide you with **60 multiple-choice graphic tests for beginning and intermediate students.**

Best wishes for continued success,

Ramiro Garcia
Ramiro Garcia

Available in English (228), Spanish (229), French (236), and German (237)

TPR IS MORE THAN COMMANDS —*AT ALL LEVELS*

CONTEE SEELY & ELIZABETH ROMIJN
Winner of the Excellence in Teaching Award

Explodes myths about the Total Physical Response:

Myth 1: TPR is limited to commands.

Myth 2: TPR is only useful at the beginning of language acquisition.

Demonstrates how you can use Professor James Asher's approach—

✔ to *overcome problems* typically encountered in the use of TPR,

✔ to teach *tenses* and *verb forms* in *any language* in 6 ways,

✔ to teach *grammar, idioms,* and *fluent discourse* in a natural way, and

✔ to help your students *tell stories* that move them into fluent speaking, reading, and writing.

Shows you how to go from zero to correct spoken fluency with TPR.

Order #	Title:
95	**TPR is More Than Commands All All Levels**

Prize-Winning!
COMPREHENSION BASED LANGUAGE LESSONS
by **Margaret S. Woodruff, Ph.D.**

**Winner of the
Paul Pimsleur Award**
(With Dr. Janet King Swaffar)
Illustrations and photographs
by Del Wieding

Here are **detailed lesson plans** for **60 hours** of **TPR Instruction** that make it **easy** for novice instructors to apply the **total physical response** approach **at any level.** The **TPR lessons** include

• **Step-by-step directions** so that instructors **in any foreign language** (including ESL) can apply comprehension training successfully.

• **Competency tests** to be given after the 10th and 30th lessons.

• **Pretested short exercises**—dozens of them to capture student interest.

• **Many photographs**

Order #290

NOTE!
To satisfy everyone, we have printed the lessons in two languages — **English** and **German**, but we have charged you only the cost of printing a single language.

TOTAL PHYSICAL RESPONSE
IN
THE FIRST YEAR
By
Dr. FRANCISCO L. CABELLO
with William Denevan

Dear Colleague:

I want to share with you the **TPR Lessons** that my high school and college students have **thoroughly enjoyed** and **retained** for weeks—even months later. My book has…

• A step-by-step script with props to conduct each class.

• A command format that students thoroughly enjoy. (Students show their understanding of the spoken language by successfully carrying out the commands given to them by the instructor. **Production** is delayed until students are ready.)

• Grammar taught implicitly through the imperative.

• Tests to evaluate student achievement.

• Now in **English, Spanish,** or **French.**

Sincerely,

Francisco Cabello, Ph.D.

Hot off the press in your choice of English (#221), Spanish (#220), or French (#222)!

How to TPR Vocabulary!

- Giant 300 page resource book, alphabetized for quick look-up.
- Yes, includes *abstractions!*

- Yes, you will discover how to TPR 2,000 vocabulary items from Level 1 and Level 2 textbooks.

Look up the word...   How to TPR it

Where   1. Pedro, stand up and run to the door. Maria, sit **where** Pedro was sitting. 2. Write the name of the country **where** you were born. 3. Touch a student who's from a country **where** the people speak Spanish (French, English).

For all ages!

Order #273

The Command Book

How to TPR 2,000 Vocabulary Items in Any Language

by STEPHEN SILVERS

How to TPR Grammar!

For Beginning, Intermediate, and Advanced Students of All Ages!

Available for English (#260), Spanish (#261), and French (#262)!

"TPR is fine for commands, but how can I use it with other grammatical features?"

Eric Schessler shows you how to apply **TPR** for **stress-free** acquisition of 50 grammatical features such as:

Abstract Nouns	Expletives	Object Pronouns	Possessive Pronouns	Simple Present
Adjectives	Future - to be going to	Past Continuous	Prepositions of Place	Singular/Plural Nouns
Adverbs	Future - Will	Past Perfect	Prepositions of Time	Subject Pronouns
Articles	Have - Present and Past	Past tense of **Be**	Present Continuous	Tag Questions
Conjunctions	Interrogative Verb forms	Possessive Case	Present Perfect	Verbs
Demonstratives	Manipulatives	and **Of** expressions	Simple Past	Wh - Questions

Laura J. Ayala

FAVORITE GAMES FOR FL - ESL CLASSES

(For All Levels and All Languages)
by
Laura Ayala & Dr. Margaret Woodruff-Wieding

Order #291

Chapter 1: Introduction

Chapter 2: Getting Started with Games
- How to get students involved
- How the games were selected or invented.

Chapter 3: Game Learning Categories
- Alphabet and Spelling
- Changing Case
- Changing Tense
- Changing Voice
- Describing Actions
- Describing Objects

Chapter 3 (Cont.)
- Getting Acquainted
- Giving Commands
- Hearing and Pronouncing
- Statements & Questions
- Negating Sentences
- Numbers and Counting
- Parts of the Body and Grooming
- Plurals and Telling How Many
- Possessive Adjectives & Belonging
- Recognizing Related Words
- Telling Time
- Using Correct Word Order.

Chapter 4: Games by Technique
- Responding to Commands
- Guessing
- Simulating
- Listing
- Categorizing
- Associating
- Sequencing
- Matching

Chapter 5: Special Materials For Games
- Objects
- Authentic Props
- Pictures
- Cards
- Stories

Chapter 6: Bibliography

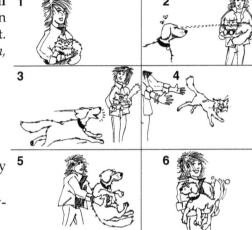

✓ **FIND the products you want from our TPR Catalog.**

✓ **E-MAIL, FAX, or MAIL the Order Form and/or School Purchase Order to us. We'll do the rest!**

TPR ORDER FORM
BOOKS • DVDs • STUDENT KITS • GAMES • ARTICLES

Sky Oaks Productions, Inc.   Since 1973
P.O. Box 1102 • Los Gatos, California, USA 95031
(408) 395-7600 • Fax: (408) 395-8440 • tprworld@aol.com • tpr–world.com

Print or Type:

Name _____ Date of Order:_____

School *or* Residence_____

Street or P.O. Box_____City_____State_____Zip_____

Country_____Phone (___)_____Fax (___)_____E-mail _____

Discover Card, Visa/MC Card No. ☐☐☐☐ ☐☐☐☐ ☐☐☐☐ ☐☐☐☐

3 Numbers on back of card: ☐☐☐   Expiration Date_____

Print the Name on the Credit Card: _____

PAGE	ORDER NO.	QUANTITY	DESCRIPTION & LANGUAGE	EACH	TOTAL

☐ **Send complete catalog plus complimentary articles.**

☐ **My Check or Purchase Order is enclosed.**

To order <u>directly</u> <u>online</u>,
go to **tpr–world.com**

Prices subject to change without notice.

Subtotal	
California residents: Add 8.25% sales tax	
USA: Add 14% for shipping & handling (minimum: $6.95)	
Outside USA: for S & H **add 39%** (minimum: 24.95)	
(U.S. Currency) Total	$

Order Form

CPSIA information can be obtained
at www.ICGtesting.com
Printed in the USA
LVHW021320061218
599450LV00019B/544/P

9 781560 180043